INTERPRETING ISAIAH

A STUDY GUIDE

Page H. Kelley

Smyth & Helwys Publishing, Inc.
6316 Peake Road
Macon, Georgia 31210-3960
1-800-747-3016

Biblical quotations, unless otherwise noted,
are from the Revised Standard Version of the Bible,
copyright 1946, 1952, c1971, 1973
by the Division of Christian Education
of the National Council of Churches of Christ in the U.S.A.,
and are used by permission.

The paper used in this publication meets the minimum requirements of
American National Standard for Information Sciences—
Permanence of Paper for Printed Library Materials.
ANSI Z39.48–1984. (alk. paper)

Library of Congress Cataloging-in-Publication Data

Kelley, Page H.
Interpreting Isaiah: a study guide / by Page H. Kelley.
Rev. ed. of : Judgment and redemption in Isaiah.
Includes bibliographical references.
ISBN 0-9628455-8-2 (alk. paper)
1. Bible. O.T. Isaiah—Criticism, interpretation, etc.
I. Kelley, Page H. Judgment and redemption in Isaiah. II. Title.
B51515.2.K39   1991
91-40043

CONTENTS

FOREWORD

Page H. Kelley, John R. Sampey Professor of Old Testament Interpretation, has taught at The Southern Baptist Theological Seminary since 1959. With devotion to his discipline and loving care for his students Dr. Kelley has unlocked the treasures of the Old Testament for generations of men and women preparing for Christian ministry. His ministry as a teacher and preacher has impacted so many others. He has devoted his life to his Lord, his family, his discipline, and thankfully to Southern Baptists.

Smyth & Helwys is pleased to present Dr. Kelley's insightful and useful treatment of key passages in the book of Isaiah. These studies are designed to assist pastors and laypersons in their understanding of the book's message of judgment and redemption. Dr. Kelley's work will be helpful to anyone wishing to hear God's contemporary word for today through the words of the anthology of prophetic oracles known as the Book of Isaiah.

Publisher
October 1991

Chapter One

ISAIAH: THE MAN AND HIS MESSAGE

The Prophet Isaiah

What do we know about Isaiah? All that we know about his personal life is found in Isaiah 1:1; 6:1–8:22; 20:1-6; 36:1–39:8; and 2 Kings 19:1–20:21. We also find some clues in Isaiah 36:1–39:8 and 2 Kings 19:1–20:21, parallel accounts of the same events near the end of Isaiah's ministry. What do these texts tell us?

The length of his ministry. According to 1:1, Isaiah prophesied during the reigns of Uzziah (783–742 B.C.), Jotham (742–735 B.C.), Ahaz (735–715 B.C.), and Hezekiah (715–687 B.C.). Isaiah's inaugural vision (6:1-13) is dated "in the year that King Uzziah died" (742 B.C.). Assuming he was perhaps around thirty years of age at that time, his birth would have occurred sometime around 770 B.C., during Uzziah's reign. The last dated events in his ministry occurred in 701 B.C., the year King Sennacherib of Assyria invaded Judah and laid siege to Jerusalem (Isa 36:1–39:8). This means that Isaiah was active during a period of at least forty years.

The circumstances of his death. There is a tradition that Isaiah was put to death by Manasseh, the evil son and successor of Hezekiah (see 2 Kgs 21:1-16). This tradition is recorded in a second-century A.D. Jewish work known as "The Martyrdom of Isaiah." It reports that the aged prophet was sawn apart by Manasseh's men after he had hid himself in a hollow tree. Hebrews 11:37 may provide a reference to the tradition about the prophet's death.

Isaiah's family. Isaiah's father was named Amoz (1:1, not to be confused with the prophet Amos). An ancient Jewish tradition states that Isaiah's father was brother to Amaziah, the father of Azariah, another name for Uzziah (see 2 Kgs 14:17-22). If this tradition is true, then Isaiah was of royal descent and thus related to the kings of Judah. There is no biblical evidence, however, to support this claim. While he may have had ready access to the presence of kings, so did many other Old Testament prophets (see 2 Sam 12:1-15; Jer 38:14-28).

Isaiah was married and his wife is referred to in 8:3 as "the prophetess." There are two explanations of why she was called a prophetess. The first is that like Miriam (see Exod 15:20-21) and Hulda (see 2 Kgs 22:14-20), she may have actually fulfilled a prophetic role of her own. Certain women also served as prophetesses during New Testament times (see Acts 21:8-9). The other suggestion is that she may have been called a prophetess simply because she was married to a prophet. There is no way of knowing which of these suggestions is correct, although the former seems more likely.

Isaiah and his wife had two sons. Like the children of Hosea (see Hos 1:2-9), Isaiah's children were given symbolic names. The first was named Shear-jashub, meaning "a remnant shall return" (7:3). It may have meant either that a remnant of Israel would repent and turn to the Lord or that a remnant would return from exile. The second child was named Maher-shalal-hash-baz, translated as "the spoil speeds, the prey hastes" (8:1-4). His name was a message of judgment against Damascus and Samaria in the crisis of 735–734 B.C. It signified the downfall of these two enemies of Judah. The names of the two sons thus conveyed messages of hope to the hard-pressed inhabitants of Jerusalem. They reminded them of God's love for them in their time of danger.

The Assyrian threat. Isaiah lived out his entire career during the period of Assyrian domination of the Middle East. The great Assyrian Empire was ruled by Tiglath-pileser from 745 to 727 B.C. This king was able to impose his will on the smaller nations around him with almost no opposition. The military campaigns waged by him and his successors kept Palestine and surrounding areas in a state of constant turmoil throughout most of Isaiah's lifetime.

Isaiah's ministry took place in the midst of four great crises. The first came in the years between 735 and 732 B.C. Around 735 B.C. Pekah, king of Israel, and Rezin, king of Syria, decided to form an alliance against the Assyrians. They tried to force Ahaz, king of Judah, to join them in this effort. When Ahaz refused they launched an attack against Jerusalem in order to unseat him (Isa 7:1; 2 Kgs 16:5).

Ahaz was young and inexperienced and the presence of invading armies on his soil filled him with panic (Isa 7:2). One day when he went out to inspect Jerusalem's water system in preparation for the expected attack upon the city, he was met by Isaiah and his son Shear-jashub (Isa 7:3). Isaiah tried but failed to win the king to a bold policy of trusting in the Lord. His message was simple, apparently too simple for Ahaz: "Trust in the Lord; be quiet and keep calm" (see Isa 7:4-9).

Disregarding the prophet's advice, Ahaz appealed directly to Tiglath-pileser for help against Pekah and Rezin (2 Kgs 16:7). His appeal was reinforced by a generous gift (2 Kgs 16:8). The Assyrian king was only too glad to oblige and stormed into the area around 732 B.C. He quickly conquered Damascus, exiled its people, and killed its king (2 Kgs 16:9). By this time Pekah had been removed from the throne in Israel and Hoshea had taken his place (2 Kgs 15:29-31). Tiglath-pileser recognized Hoshea as the new Israelite king and made him his vassal. The northern kingdom of Israel had now been incorporated into the vast Assyrian Empire. It would never again regain its independence.

Ahaz's appeal to Tiglath-pileser enabled him to remain on the throne in Jerusalem, but only at the cost of heavy taxation and continuing subjection to the Assyrians (2 Kgs 16:10-18). His failure to follow Isaiah's advice proved to be a costly blunder both for him and for the southern kingdom of Judah.

The second crisis that occurred during Isaiah's career was the fall of Israel to the Assyrians in 722 B.C. Although Judah was not directly involved, nevertheless, the final collapse of Israel placed the Assyrians on her northern frontier, where they continued to threaten her existence for the next century or so. The downfall of Israel, therefore, constituted a crisis that Isaiah could not afford to overlook as he addressed the people of Judah.

The immediate cause of Israel's downfall was King Hoshea's revolt against Shalmaneser V, the son and successor of Tiglath-pileser and the ruler of the Assyrian Empire from 727 to 722 B.C. Hoshea revolted against Assyria around 726 B.C., apparently expecting to receive support from the Egyptians (Isa 30:1–31:9; 2 Kgs 17:4). Shalmaneser attacked Israel the following year, took Hoshea prisoner, and laid siege to Samaria. Isaiah used this occasion to warn the nation of its peril (Isa 9:8–10:4; 17:1-11; 28:1-4). His warning went unheeded and after a siege of three years Samaria fell to the Assyrians in 722 B.C. (2 Kgs 17:5-6). After this took place, Judah was left to face the Assyrians alone.

The third crisis during Isaiah's ministry came in 711 B.C. In 715 B.C., while Sargon was engaged in battle elsewhere, rebellion against Assyria broke out again in southern Palestine. It was centered in the city-state of Ashdod, whose king had apparently received offers of help from Egypt and Ethiopia.

King Ahaz of Judah had by now been replaced by Hezekiah (715–687 B.C.). The king of Ashdod sought the support of Judah and other neighboring states against Assyria. Isaiah advised Hezekiah against giving such support, believing that in the end it would be disastrous for Judah (Isa 20:1-6).

By 711 B.C. Sargon moved to crush this rebellion. When his troops reached Ashdod, its rebel king took refuge in Egypt, only to be captured and handed over to the Assyrians. Sargon left a victory memorial at Ashdod celebrating his success in crushing this rebellion. He set up a black basalt pillar inscribed with a glowing account of his victory. (Some of the pieces of this pillar were discovered in 1963 at the site of ancient Ashdod.) It is not known how much Hezekiah became involved in the Ashdod rebellion. He apparently suffered some reprisals from the Assyrians when they came to crush the rebellion (Isa 22:1-14), but did not lose his freedom.

The fourth and most serious crisis during Isaiah's prophetic ministry came in 701 B.C. The king of Assyria was now Sennacherib (705–681 B.C.). When Sennacherib succeeded Sargon, he was faced with widespread rebellion throughout the Assyrian Empire. This included a full-scale revolt by Hezekiah, king of Judah. This time

Hezekiah seems to have had the support of Isaiah in his rebellion against Assyria, contrary to the prophet's stance on earlier occasions. Some biblical scholars see Isaiah 24–27 as a celebration of the expulsion of the Assyrian troops from Jerusalem at this time.

Sennacherib moved in 701 B.C. to crush this rebellion. One of his armies marched down the Philistine coast and defeated the Egyptians. A second army moved across Samaria and approached Jerusalem from the north (Isa 10:28-34). Sennacherib claims to have destroyed forty-six cities of Judah during this campaign. Concerning Judah's king he wrote, "Hezekiah I made a prisoner in Jerusalem, his royal residence, like a bird in a cage." Isaiah 1:8 probably refers to the devastation of the land at this time, as it speaks of Jerusalem being left "like a booth in a vineyard, like a lodge in a cucumber field, like a besieged city."

Isaiah's role in these events is described in Isaiah 36:1–37:38 and in the parallel passages in 2 Kings 18:13–19:37. The prophet was vindicated in his words of encouragement to Hezekiah when a deadly plague struck the Assyrian army and caused it to withdraw from Jerusalem as suddenly as it had come (Isa 37:33-37; 2 Kgs 19:32-36). Apparently Isaiah did not engage in any other prophetic activity after these events. The remainder of the book (chapters 40–66) treats events that took place more than a century and a half after his death.

By way of summary, we may note that Isaiah's prophetic ministry was divided into four periods:

1. From the death of Uzziah to the early years of Ahaz, 742–735 B.C.
2. From the Syro-Ephraimitic crisis to the fall of Samaria, 735–722 B.C.
3. The period of Assyrian aggression against Judah, 722–701 B.C.
4. From Sennacherib's siege of Jerusalem, 701 B.C., to the death of Isaiah.

The danger from within. In addition to the danger from outside her borders, Judah was faced with an even greater danger from within. It was the danger from her own moral and spiritual decay.

The people to whom Isaiah ministered were laboring under four false assumptions:

1. Through the Sinai covenant God had bound himself to Israel with ties that could not be broken.
2. Israel was fully discharging her covenant obligations by simply observing the ritual of cult and sacrifice.
3. The Day of the Lord would be an automatic day of triumph for God and for Israel.
4. No matter how difficult matters became, God would never allow Jerusalem to be captured or destroyed. There was, so they thought, a magic ring around the city, and its inhabitants.

The prophet ruthlessly attacked each of these assumptions. God was not bound by the covenant, once Israel had broken it. What he demanded was not sacrifice, but justice, mercy, and faith. Since these qualities were lacking in Israel, she could expect the Day of the Lord to be a day of judgment and destruction. Even Jerusalem, the site of God's sanctuary, would not escape the judgment.

Isaiah's Contributions to Israel's Religion

Isaiah taught that God was directing all history in accordance with his purpose of establishing his rule on earth. The classic statement of this truth is in chapter 10. When the prophet spoke these words, the Assyrians seemed to be invincible. However, he believed it was God and not the Assyrians who was in charge of history. Though they seemed to have a lot of rope, nevertheless the end of the rope was in the hands of God.

More than any prophet, Isaiah stressed the holiness of God. At the time of his call, he heard this holiness being celebrated in the song of the seraphim (Isa 6:3). From then on, his favorite designation for the Lord was "the Holy One of Israel," a title used some thirty times throughout the book (see, for example, 1:4; 10:20; 12:6; 17:7; 31:3; etc.).

Isaiah warned against the folly of human pride. He regarded the ultimate sin of the nations as that of pride in their own power, pride in their own wisdom, and pride in their own achievements. He spoke of the coming day of the Lord as a day when the pride of the nations would be judged and everything lifted up would be brought low (see 2:12-17). Assyria, drunk with its own power and might, would be humbled in the sight of all nations (see 10:12-19). It was the Lord's purpose to crush all monuments to human pride and to stand alone as the Exalted and Holy One of Israel (see 16:67; 47:1, 8).

As a corollary to the Lord's hatred of human pride, Isaiah taught that he made himself available to the meek and lowly. This is perhaps best stated in 57:15:

> For thus says the high and lofty One who inhabits eternity, whose name is Holy: "I dwell in the high and holy place, and also with him who is of a contrite and humble spirit, to revive the spirit of the humble, and to revive the heart of the contrite."

Loving God always involves loving one's neighbor. One of Isaiah's basic teachings was that true service to God consisted of service to mankind. This applied especially to deeds of justice and mercy performed on behalf of earth's poor and oppressed, its homeless, its widows, and its orphans. These were the defenseless members of society for whom the political structure offered little protection and little support.

Isaiah's contemporaries believed that the true service of God consisted of acts of worship performed at a central sanctuary with a duly ordained priesthood offering the appointed sacrifices. They also believed that they were being fully obedient to God when they participated in such services of worship. To them right ritual was of far greater significance than right living.

Isaiah had an entirely different view of what it meant to be rightly related to God. To him true worship included far more than offering proper sacrifices and keeping holy days (see 1:11, 14). He taught that one who would be truly pleasing to God must "learn to do good; seek justice, correct oppression; defend the fatherless, plead for the widow"

(1:17). What God desired most from his people was justice and right-eousness (5:7). Without these, all acts of worship lost their significance.

Perhaps more than any other Hebrew prophet, Isaiah presented faith as the believer's only adequate response to God. In crisis after crisis in the life of his people, he proclaimed faith in God as the only alternative to frustration and defeat. This was the heart of his counsel to Ahaz in 735 B.C. (see 7:9) and to Hezekiah in 701 B.C. (see 28:16; 30:15). Isaiah felt that these kings' feverish efforts to strengthen the defenses of Jerusalem, together with their endless appeals to foreign powers for help, indicated an attitude of unbelief. They were guilty of placing the power of man above the power of God. Faith in God with humble obedience to his will was the only road to social and political stability.

More than any other prophet, Isaiah was responsible for the development of the messianic hope in the Old Testament. He was one of the first, if not the first, of the prophets to link the coming of the Messiah and the dream of an ideal age of righteousness and peace (see 2:2-4; 9:2-7; 11:1-9).

The messianic hope of the Old Testament, to which Isaiah contributed so much, consisted of the belief that in days to come God would raise up a righteous king from the line of David to rule over his people. Righteousness and peace would characterize the rule of this messianic king and his dominion would extend to the ends of the earth. This hope tended to shine brightest when Israel's circumstances were the darkest. Perhaps this helps to explain why it was so strong against the background of the Assyrian threat of the eighth century B.C.

Isaiah's messianic expectation was born largely of his disappointment in the kings that ruled Judah during his lifetime. In a famous trilogy of messianic passages, he speaks of Messiah's birth (7:10-16), of his accession to the throne (9:2-7), and of his righteous rule (11:1-9).

The impression one gains from a close study of these passages is that Isaiah expected these events to take place in his own day and age. He had no way of knowing that their fulfillment would be postponed for another seven centuries. When in the fullness of time the Messiah did come, the glories of his kingdom far outshone even the fondest expectations of the prophet.

The Unity of the Book of Isaiah

Is the Book of Isaiah the work of a single author, Isaiah the son of Amoz, whose ministry occurred during the last half of the eighth century B.C.? This was the prevailing view until relatively recent times.

This is still the view of a number of Old Testament scholars. The arguments cited in support of this position are

1. the witness of the New Testament (see John 12:38-41; Rom 9:27-33; 10:16-21);
2. the witness of ancient Jewish writings outside the Old Testament (see Eccl 49:17-25);
3. the witness of Isaiah 1:1, which seems to indicate that Isaiah was the author of the entire book; and
4. the unity that pervades the entire prophecy.

Other scholars, however, maintain that these arguments are not sufficient to settle the question of authorship. These scholars are not at all certain that Isaiah wrote chapters 40–66. Those who study these chapters find themselves in the latter part of the sixth century B.C., almost two centuries later than the time of Isaiah, the son of Amos.

This fact is acknowledged by almost all Old Testament scholars. Differences arise, however, in the way this fact is explained. Some argue that Isaiah himself wrote these chapters in his old age. These hold that under the inspiration of the Holy Spirit he foresaw in minute detail events that were to occur some two centuries later. He foresaw the time when Israel would be exiled to Babylon and later delivered by the hand of Cyrus. Although prediction forms a legitimate part of prophecy, this is not the primary role of Old Testament prophets. More often than not they were called messengers of a contemporary word from God for their audience, not predictors of events hundreds of years in the future.

Most Old Testament scholars believe that chapters 40–66 were written by an unknown prophet, or prophets, of the exilic period. This anonymous author is usually designated as Deutero-Isaiah, or Second Isaiah. This must not be interpreted to mean that he was actually named Isaiah. It merely means that he was a later disciple of Isaiah and that his writings were included in the same scroll with Isaiah's writings. What this amounts to is a theory of joint authorship.

What are the arguments advanced in favor of this view?

The principle of prophetic analogy. Since the prophets always spoke directly to their own times, of what interest would it have been to the contemporaries of Isaiah to hear of Babylon and the campaigns of Cyrus? Israel's enemy in the eighth century B.C. was Assyria, not Babylon. A good rule of thumb for dating a prophecy is that it must be earlier than that which it predicts, but later than that which it presupposes. Chapters 40–66 presuppose that Israel is in exile, but predict that the exile will soon be over and that Israel will be restored to her land. These chapters should, therefore, be dated later than 587 B.C., but earlier than 538 B.C.

The silence of the other pre-exilic prophets. If chapters 40–66 had been written by Isaiah during the eighth century, they presumably would have been available to the prophets of the seventh and sixth centuries—Zephaniah, Habakkuk, Jeremiah, and Ezekiel. These prophets would then have understood perfectly what God purposed to do when he delivered his people into the hand of the Babylonians. There is no indication, however, that any of them had ever heard of these prophecies. Those who assume that they were written by Isaiah of Jerusalem, must also assume they were kept secret for almost two centuries.

The historical background. Chapters 40–48 presuppose a situation prior to the fall of Babylon. The Jews were in captivity in the land of Babylon (42:22, 24; 48:20). Cyrus had entered upon the stage of history (44:48; 45:1). He had already made rapid conquests in the east and northwest (41:2-3, 25; 46:11). He was about to challenge and overthrow the power of Babylon (46:2; 47:1-15; 48:14). These references to Cyrus's conquests indicate that he had already conquered

Astyages of Media and Croesus of Sardis. This suggests a date after 546 B.C. but before 539 B.C.

The historical situation as presented in chapters 49–55 is somewhat different. The absence of any reference to Cyrus seems to imply that he had already taken Babylon. The proclamation of liberty had been issued (48:20), but the Jews had not yet left Babylon to return to Jerusalem (49:8-9). Nevertheless, the time of deliverance was near (51:14; 52:1-6, 11). Tidings to this effect were being published, and the long-awaited day was about to dawn (55:12-13). All of these considerations suggest a date for these chapters just prior to 538 B.C.

While in chapters 40–55 the Jews are in exile in Babylon, in chapters 56–66 they are once more in Jerusalem. It is likely, therefore, that the latter chapters were written after some of the exiles had returned to Jerusalem. Some scholars have even attributed these chapters to a "Third Isaiah," but others argue that they were written by the same prophet who wrote 40–55.

To abandon this view of the unity of 40–66 leaves one with the problem of two great prophets who were almost identical in their thoughts, attitudes, language, and forms of poetic expression. Some would argue, therefore, that after Second-Isaiah had written chapters 40–55 in Babylon, he returned to Jerusalem with the freed exiles in 538 B.C. and wrote the concluding chapters shortly thereafter. However, one must not rule out the possibility that other anonymous writings were incorporated into the final form of the book. This would help to account for the wide diversity of materials found in chapters 56–66.

The language, literary style, and form. The difference between the language, style, and form of chapters 1–39 and 40–66 is so great that one is aware of it even in translation. Those who can read the original Hebrew are made much more aware of this difference. When readers pass from 1–39 to 40–66, they feel they have closed the book of one author and opened that of another.

Theological ideas. Reference has already been made to the contributions of Isaiah to the religious thought of Israel. Second Isaiah made some unique contributions of his own. Because of his portrayal of God as Creator and Redeemer, his clear statement on the idea of vicarious suffering, his teaching concerning the universal purpose of God, and his ideal of the love and compassion of God, he has been called the "evangelist of the Old Testament." The difference between the Messiah of 9:1-6 and 11:1-9 and the Servant of the Lord in chapters 40–55 points to two authors rather than one.

In conclusion, the evidence cited above has convinced most scholars that the Book of Isaiah came from two or more prophets covering a span of approximately two centuries. Few books of the Bible went through such an extended period of composition. It is possible for scholars to disagree in their views regarding the unity of the book, but still agree that all of it is the inspired Word of God.

> The grass withers, the flower fades;
> but the word of our God will stand for ever.   —Isaiah 40:8

Chapter Two

ISAIAH'S CALL AND COMMISSION
6:1-13

In all the literature of the Old Testament there is nothing quite like Isaiah 6. Here the law, the prophets, and the psalms all converge. We are reminded of the law by the vision of the temple, the altar, and the burning coals. We are at the heart of the prophetic literature as we study the account of Isaiah's call. This account also contains the two basic elements of the psalms-praise and petition.

This chapter describes Isaiah's encounter with the living God. There are three aspects of this encounter that are emphasized: (1) Isaiah saw God; (2) Isaiah saw himself; and (3) Isaiah saw a world in need.

Isaiah's Vision of God (6:1-4)

This vision is dated "in the year that King Uzziah died." This good king had reigned approximately forty years in Judah (783–742 B.C.). Second Kings 15:1-7 and 2 Chronicles 26 give a summary account of his extraordinary achievements. Isaiah had never lived under the reign of another king.

Since kingship is more or less alien to our culture, it is difficult for us to appreciate the significance of the king in ancient society. He was like a father to his subjects. From him blessings and strength went out to the whole nation. For this reason the death of Uzziah must have brought deep grief to the people of Judah. Perhaps we might draw an analogy between their consternation and that of the American people at the news of the assassination of President Kennedy.

On that day Isaiah made his way into the temple and there received a vision that transformed his life. In the year that King Uzziah died, Isaiah saw the divine King who never dies. The throne in Judah was empty, but the throne in heaven was occupied by one eternal King whose glory filled the earth. Judah's kings might come and go in an endless procession, but this King would reign forever. His throne was lifted above all earthly thrones.

Around the throne were seraphim, each having six wings. These symbolized reverence, modesty, and service. It is believed by some that these strange creatures were fiery flying serpents, similar to the serpents that were carved on the thrones of the pharaohs of Egypt. The seraphim were singing in antiphony. The theme of their song was the praise of God's holiness.

As a result of this experience, the holiness of the Lord became a dominant theme in Isaiah's preaching. His favorite term for God was "the Holy One of Israel," a term that appears about thirty times in the entire book (1:4; 5:19, 24; etc.). Isaiah knew that Judah's very existence depended on her attitude toward the holiness of God.

To say that God is holy means first of all that he is God and not man (cf. Hos 11:9). A modern theologian has suggested this axiom: "The holy God is the wholly Other." Let us note, however, that as Isaiah stood in the presence of the thrice-holy God he was not so much aware of his creatureliness as of his defilement. Holiness for him had taken on a new dimension. He feared God not merely because he was a human being but because he was a sinner. He had come to a deeper understanding of the moral significance of holiness.

Isaiah's Vision of Himself (6:5-7)

Isaiah saw God and in the light of that vision he saw himself. Those who come close to God have an increased awareness of his holiness and of their own sinfulness. Isaiah had never realized the depth of his sin and depravity until he saw the measure of God's holiness.

Isaiah saw himself as a man of unclean lips. Why was he so concerned about his lips? Why was his consciousness of defilement focused here rather than elsewhere? This may indicate that he knew even before this experience that God wanted him to be a prophet, a man of the spoken word. As the messenger of God, his lips must be cleansed and undefiled. Even the Accadians and the Egyptians caused their prophets to submit to certain mouth purification rites before they delivered the oracles of the gods. Religious teachers or preachers will be seriously handicapped in speaking for God if their lips have not been cleansed and prepared for this task.

Isaiah saw himself as a man of unclean lips dwelling in the midst of a people of unclean lips. Sin affects not only the individual but also the society in which that individual lives. The fact that society is accountable to God for its actions has often been overlooked. We tend to emphasize individual sin and guilt almost to the exclusion of any notion of corporate guilt. The lack of a sense of corporate responsibility has led to the adoption of a double code of ethics, one for the group and another for the individual. As members of a group we permit ourselves to do things we would never do if acting alone.

An illustration of what can happen when men disavow personal responsibility for corporate evil is provided by Nazi Germany. When Adolph Eichmann stood trial for the slaughter of six million Jews, he based his defense on the claim that "where there is no personal responsibility there is no guilt." Such a plea does not release us from our responsibility for the sins of the society in which we live.

Isaiah's response to the vision of God was that of a person brought face to face with death. From his lips there burst forth an agonizing cry of despair, "Woe is me, for I am undone!" John R. Sampey used to translate this, "Woe is me, for I am a goner!" For one such as Isaiah to look into the face of God meant certain death. But Isaiah had failed to make allowance for the mercy of God.

God heard his lament and cleansed his lips and forgave his sin. The manner in which this was done is significant. One of the seraphim flew to the altar to take a burning coal from the fire. He pressed this against Isaiah's lips and cauterized them. This must have been painful to endure, even in a vision.

There is no painless cure for sin. It must be dealt with drastically. Forgiveness must always be secured at the price of suffering and death. This was why the Son of God had to go to the cross.

This account of Isaiah's call rebukes our age for its easygoing attitude toward sin. All too often it is lightly treated from the pulpit and lightly regarded in the pew. By our moral and ethical ambivalence we have encouraged sinners to indulge in excuses, pretense, and self-pity. Edmund Fuller has suggested that our advice to the woman taken in adultery and brought to Christ would be, "Neither do I condemn you; go and sin some more."

It must be said that a morbid sense of sin with no corresponding trust in God is the most destructive and disintegrating thing there is. It destroys all happiness on earth and provides none anywhere else. But a recognition of one's guilt which is accompanied by repentance and faith leads to forgiveness, peace, and fullness of life.

Isaiah's Vision of a World in Need (6:8-13)

The center and climax of Isaiah's call comes in verse 8. The consequence of his being cleansed and forgiven was something unique among the prophets. Instead of pleading his inadequacy, as Moses and Jeremiah had done, he volunteered to be sent out even before he knew what his task would be.

Isaiah was so overwhelmed with a sense of gratitude that he was ready to place his life entirely in the hands of God. God had taken care of his past; he could have his future. It has always been thus. Those who have been forgiven much, love much. The measure of our willingness to serve is always the measure of our gratitude to God for forgiveness.

The words "Here am I! Send me" appear as only two words in Hebrew. They were Isaiah's response to God's challenge, "Whom shall I send, and who will go for us?" The heavenly court had been in session. A verdict of guilty had been handed down against Judah. God needed a messenger to deliver this verdict to the sinful and rebellious nation. Isaiah's urgent response suggests he was afraid someone else might be chosen. One can almost see him, waving his hand and shouting to gain God's attention.

Since Isaiah did not know the nature of his mission he was simply making himself available. He would go wherever God sent him. Only after he made this commitment did God call *him*. Only after he had said "Send me" did God say "Go."

Is this not the way God always works? He wants us to make ourselves available to him. It is not our ability so much as our availability that matters to him. Some will not say "Send me" for fear that God will say "Go."

And God said,

> Go, and say to this people:
> "Hear and hear [i.e., keep on hearing],
>   but do not understand;
> see and see [i.e., keep on seeing],
>   but do not perceive.
> Make the heart of this people fat,
>   and their ears heavy,
>   and shut their eyes;
> lest they see with their eyes,
> and hear with their ears,
>   and understand with their hearts,
>   and turn and be healed."   —vv. 9-10

We must not interpret these words as the intended or desired result of the prophet's preaching. God was saying that in view of the rebellious nature of his listeners this was the inevitable result.

It is a sobering experience to realize that our preaching and teaching will crystalize the character and seal the destiny of many of those who listen to us. This thought was in the mind of Paul when he wrote, "For we are the aroma of Christ to God among those who are being saved and among those who are perishing, to one a fragrance from death to death, to the other a fragrance from life to life. Who is sufficient for these things?" (2 Cor 2:15-16).

Who is sufficient indeed? Isaiah cried out, "How long, O Lord?" This cry is familiar to us from the psalms of lament (cf. Pss 13:2; 74:10; 79:5; 89:46). It is the cry of a troubled soul. And well might one be troubled when he faces a task like Isaiah's. If one listens closely to missionaries and pastors today, he will hear them also saying, "How long, O Lord?"

God's answer does not specify any time limit. Isaiah is to continue until his job is finished. He is to continue preaching until the nation he loves lies in ruins.

Verse 13 has been interpreted in various ways. The traditional interpretation is that it contains the prophet's doctrine of a saved remnant that springs into existence as by a divine miracle. Even though the devastation is total, there is still a ray of hope. As a felled tree retains a spark of life in its stump and begins to grow again, so in Judah there would be left a righteous remnant through whom the purposes of God would ultimately be realized.

Since the closing words, "The holy seed is its stump," are lacking in the Septuagint, many regard them as a later addition. They appear in the Dead Sea Scroll of Isaiah, however, and were probably omitted from the Septuagint by error. The idea of a righteous remnant seems to be an integral part of Isaiah's theology, dating back to the very beginning of his prophetic ministry.

Chapter Three

GOD'S JUDGMENT AGAINST JUDAH
1:1–5:25

In keeping with the commission given in chapter 6, the early messages of Isaiah were messages of doom. With minor exceptions, most of the material in chapters 1–5 belongs to this early part of his ministry.

God's Case against His People (1:1-31)

Verses 1-9 treat Judah's rebellion and its dire consequences. Her sin is basically that of ingratitude (vv. 2-4). She is accused of showing less gratitude than an ox or an ass that feeds from its master's crib. Her sin is all the more serious because God has cared for her as a father would care for his sons. The fourfold address in verse 4—nation, people, off-spring, sons—is a progressively personal way to show God's relationship to his people.

The consequences of Judah's rebellion are described in verses 59. Judah is like a rebellious child, beaten until his body is completely covered with bruises and wounds. Still he is unwilling to turn his evil ways. These verses emphasize the suicidal nature of Judah's course of action.

The desolation pictured in these verses has led many scholars to date them in 701 B.C. It was then that Sennacherib invaded Judah and besieged Jerusalem. According to the annals of this king, he took forty-six of the walled towns in Judah and shut Hezekiah up in Jerusalem like a bird in a cage.

The setting in verses 10-20 is clearly not the same as in the pre-ceding passage. Here the temple is thronged with worshipers, and sacrifices are plentiful. This was clearly a time of peace when pilgrimages could be made to the temple.

In these verses the prophet declares the worthlessness of ritual that is divorced from righteousness. He probably spoke these words on a feast day when the temple was crowded with worshipers. His words are addressed to the rulers of Sodom and to the people of Gomorrah (v. 10). These are figurative terms for Judah and Jerusalem. The prophet could not have chosen more offensive terms with which to address his hearers.

The prophet declares the worthlessness of sacrifices (v. 11), solemn assemblies (vv. 13-14), and prayers (v. 15), so long as Judah is defiled. She is commanded to cleanse herself, to abandon her evil ways, to learn to do good, and to protect the defenseless members of society (vv. 16-17).

Repentance is her only alternative to destruction (vv. 18-20). Here God is described as a judge who summons the accused to appear before his bench. Verse 18 has often been interpreted as a gracious promise or invitation. One commentator has called it "that tender, that incredible evangel," likening it to John 3:16. This interpretation is probably wrong. This verse should probably be interpreted as an indignant question: "If your sins are like scarlet, can they be judged to be as white as snow? If they are as crimson, can they be as white as snow?" The answer, of course, would be an emphatic no. Israel herself must choose between life and death, between the blessing and the curse (vv. 19-20).

In verses 21-23 Jerusalem is compared to a maiden who has lost her virtue. In the past she was known for her justice and righteousness, but now she has become a spiritual harlot. She has become like alloyed silver and adulterated wine. The greed for gain has corrupted her rulers, who no longer defend the fatherless or the widows.

Verses 24-28 contain both promise and threat. The Mighty One of Israel will take vengeance on rebels, but those who repent will be redeemed. The dross and alloy will be smelted away and Jerusalem will once more be called the city of righteousness.

The closing verses of this chapter constitute an attack on Judah's pagan worship. The oaks and the gardens (v. 29) were associated with

Baal worship. Those who delight in oaks will become like oaks—with withered leaves! Those who choose gardens will become like gardens— without water!

The sin of idolatry brings its own destruction (v. 31). The strong are to be identified with rebels and idolaters. They shall become tow— the fiber of flax or other similar plants—which was used to start fires. Their evil deeds constitute the spark that ignites the tow. Sinners are set on fire by their own sins and nothing can quench the fire. This is Isaiah's way of saying the wages of sin is death.

The Vision of Universal Peace (2:1-5)

This same prophecy in a slightly longer form is found in Micah 4:1-7. Since Isaiah and Micah were contemporaries, it is impossible to know which one of them was the original author of these words. It is even possible that each was repeating an anonymous poem that was current in their day.

Four conclusions can be drawn from this eschatological poem:

1. Universal peace is possible only in a world in which the sovereignty of God is recognized.
2. Universal peace rests upon no human program but upon obedience to the revealed will of God.
3. Universal peace will be effective only when there is total disarmament.
4. Universal peace will be accompanied by freedom from want and freedom from fear (cf. Mic 4:4).

Of special interest in this poem is the concept that war is "learned." It is not inevitable in the affairs of nations. Of course, there are revolutionary philosophies that teach that the nature of things is to be at war. Communism, for example, believes in the eternal conflict of the classes. It holds that only through violent revolution can justice be achieved.

Christianity teaches the exact opposite. The God of the Bible is a God of peace. His covenant with us is a covenant of peace—peace on earth and good will. The Lord of the Christian is the Prince of peace. The Christian, therefore, believes that war is not inevitable and that one day nations shall not learn war any more.

It is significant that this prophecy of universal peace has been inscribed on the United Nations Plaza in New York. There one reads

> The nations shall beat their swords into plowshares,
> and their spears into pruning hooks:
> nation shall not lift up sword against nation,
> neither shall they learn war any more.

Lord, hasten that day!

The Day of the Lord (2:6-22)

The "day of the Lord" is a term that occurs often in the Old Testament, especially in the prophets. It sometimes appears in abbreviated form as "the day," or "that day" (cf. vv. 11, 12, 17, 20). It refers to those times and seasons in history when God intervenes to judge the wicked and to save the righteous. When all the references to this day are considered, it can be seen that the aspect of judgment is far more prominent than that of deliverance and salvation (cf. Zeph 1:15).

The day of the Lord is necessary because the house of Jacob had become rich, idolatrous, and proud (vv. 6-11). Isaiah announced a day when God would judge everything that is high and exalted (vv. 12-17). The Lord alone would be exalted in that day.

The emphasis is upon the word *alone.* Everything high and exalted on this earth advances toward the day when it will be destroyed. The works of human beings—even the highest works—are not eternal. Of course, we often make the mistake of regarding them as eternal. But in this world of change and decay, only God is eternal. Human beings should never make the mistake of conferring on that which their fingers have made a highness which belongs to God. Only those who see the limitations of all human greatness can recognize the greatness of God.

These words of Isaiah must be seen against the background of the rising power of Assyria. Small countries were being swallowed up right and left, and yet Isaiah had the faith to believe that "the pride of men shall be brought low." He believed so firmly in the power of God that he did not allow himself to become fascinated by the power of Assyria or any other nation.

Verses 18-22 describe the destruction of all idols and the utter confusion of all idolaters. Their cry will be, "Back to the caves!" In vain they will attempt to find a hiding place from the Lord.

During World War II an American ship, with all lights out, was crossing the Pacific at night. Suddenly there loomed up in the darkness ahead the shadow of a large Japanese ship. Seconds later the decks of the American ship were bathed in light as the enemy sailors turned on their powerful searchlights. In that agonizing moment some of the American sailors tried to claw holes in the steel decks in order to hide from the blinding light. Even so will idolaters seek to hide from the brightness of God when he rises to terrify the earth (v. 19).

Verse 22 is an echo of Genesis 2:7. The Old Testament concept of human existence is that we are but dust animated by the breath of God. One of the psalms states, "When thou takest away their breath, they die and return to their dust" (Ps 104:29; cf. Eccl 12:7).

The answer to the question "For of what account is he?" is that human beings are of no account. Of course, this must be understood against the background of Isaiah's description of the people of his day. They were filled with pride and self-exaltation, people who lived as though the Lord were not on his throne. Psalm 8 deals with this same question but with different results.

Anarchy and the Collapse of Society (3:1–4:1)

A good heading for this section would be "The Crisis in Leadership." The prophet pictures a time when competent leaders are removed and the administration of the country falls into the hands of incompetent weaklings. This section should perhaps be dated near the beginning of the reign of Ahaz. According to 2 Kings 16:2, he was only twenty years old when he took the throne. There may be an allusion to his youthfulness in verses 4 and 12.

Five groups of leaders are scheduled to be removed from their places of responsibility. They are the military commanders, the judges, the elders, the counselors, and the prophets. These were those who should have been the pillars of society.

Their removal results in social anarchy. No one will assume the responsibility of ruling in their stead (vv. 6-7).

The low state to which Jerusalem has sunk is described in verses 8-12. The emphasis throughout this section is that Jerusalem has no one but herself to blame for the sorry state in which she finds herself. It has been said that a nation always gets the kind of rulers it deserves. What does this say about the political situation in America today?

God enters into controversy with the leaders of his people in verses 13-15. They are condemned for their injustice and for their exploitation of the poor. These words of Isaiah remind us of the prophet Amos (cf. Amos 2:7; 8:4). Both of these prophets picture God as the defender of the helpless poor who had no one to plead their case.

The climactic step in the collapse of society is the downfall of the first ladies of Jerusalem (3:16 to 4:1). In this passage Isaiah mentions no fewer than twenty-four items of dress or of makeup used by the women of Jerusalem. While he may have been a man's man, he certainly knew a lot about women!

Isaiah knew that a nation's character is largely determined by the quality of its womanhood. If they are cruel, or careless, or unwomanly, then the nation's well-being is threatened. The integrity of its womanhood is the last bulwark of any nation.

The Glorious Future of God's Purified People (4:2-6)

This prophecy is introduced by the eschatological formula, "in that day." In that future day the soil of Israel would become exceedingly productive and fruitful (v. 2). All of those who survived the time of judgment would be holy (v. 3), consecrated to the Lord. This would occur when the Lord had washed away their filth and purified them in the fires of judgment (v. 4).

Then the glory of the Lord would cover Zion and her holy assemblies like a great pavilion. It would be like the pillar of cloud and the pillar of fire that went before the Israelites in the wilderness (cf. Exod 13:21-22). The "glory" of the Lord is used in the Old Testament to describe his "tabernacling" presence with his people. The glory both conceals God and reveals him. It reveals enough to confirm men's faith and conceals enough to stimulate their reverence and quicken their devotion.

The Song of the Vineyard (5:1-7)

It is possible that Isaiah posed as a minstrel when he sang this song. This would have been an effective way to catch the attention of the crowds on their way to the Temple. Perhaps they were on their way to attend a harvest festival, such as the Feast of Tabernacles. Isaiah appealed to their own interests as he sang of the care he had given his vineyard.

It has been said that five things are necessary for good farming. They are (1) the selection of good soil; (2) careful cultivation of the soil; (3) the selection of good seed; (4) protection of the crop during the growing season; and (5) adequate preparation for harvesting and storing the crop.

The prophet describes himself as having followed all these steps. First, he chose a fertile field. The Hebrew language is almost completely devoid of adjectives. In order to express the idea of a fertile field, it employs a phrase which, translated, literally means "a hill, the son of fatness."

The prophet then spaded up the soil in his field and cleared it of stones. Removing the stones is an essential part of farming in Palestine. The fields are littered with stones of all sizes. In the fall of 1963, I traveled from Jerusalem down to Hebron. All along the highway the hillsides were terraced with stones that had been gathered out of the fields. The ancient rabbis had a legend that told how at creation God sent the angel Gabriel with a bag of stones to be scattered over the face of the earth. But alas! When he passed over Palestine the bag burst and all the stones spilled out!

The prophet secured the choicest vines for his vineyard. The Hebrew even uses a special word to emphasize the rare quality of the vines.

The crop must be protected from marauders, human and otherwise. So the owner built a tower in the midst of the vineyard. Palestinian farmers still protect their crops in this manner. The towers are usually built of stone, but occasionally one sees a lookout perched atop a platform supported by wooden stilts. The modern lookout usually carries a firearm of some sort.

The prophet was so confident of an abundant harvest that he hewed out a wine vat in the midst of the vineyard. In almost all the fields there are outcrops of limestone where wine vats could be hewn out. With the primitive tools available, this was a painstaking task.

But all the planning and labor were useless because the harvest was a failure. Instead of grapes the vineyard produced stinking fruit.

Having described his disappointment in his vineyard, the prophet then turned to his audience and asked them to judge between him and his vineyard. Was he to be blamed for the crop failure? Had he overlooked some detail in caring for his vineyard?

The audience probably responded with a resounding no! The fault was not with the prophet but rather with the vineyard.

The prophet then described the measures he planned to take against his vineyard. At first sight, one is impressed with the mildness of these measures. He doesn't propose to go in and chop down the vines. He simply removes his protection from the vineyard and ceases to care for it. Its walls are broken down. It is no longer pruned or hoed. No rains fall upon it. These, however, are in actuality very drastic measures. A vineyard or an orchard ceases to yield fruit if it is not cared for.

In one of my student pastorates I often visited a deacon who had an apple orchard. The orchard was well tended and the apple-laden trees were a delight to behold. The deacon died, however, and there was no one left to care for the orchard. Today the trees are still there but they no longer bear fruit.

The prophet applied the parable of the vineyard to God's relationship to Israel. Because Israel had failed to bear the fruit that God had expected of her, he was going to withdraw his protection and care. He would abandon Israel to her own fate.

How dreadful it is for God to withdraw his presence from his people! The saddest day in any person's life is when God says, "Thy will be done."

The vineyard of the Lord was the house of Israel. From his vineyard he had expected a harvest of justice and righteousness (v. 7). Instead, it had produced bloodshed and an outcry. There is a play on words in both instances here. He had looked for justice, but behold, distress; he had looked for right, but behold, a riot.

The word "cry" is a legal term. It refers to the anguished appeal of one who is being oppressed. It could be translated "foul play!" With such a cry a person appealed to the legal authorities for help. When this cry was ignored by the administrators of justice on earth it ascended to the Lord, who was the protector of the helpless and the oppressed.

Isaiah's Six Woes upon Judah (5:8-25)

Woe to the greedy land-grabbers (vv. 8-10). Those are condemned who acquire house after house and field after field until they are left neighborless on their estates. While Isaiah does not specifically state that this was done through dishonest means, his contemporary indicates that this was indeed so (Mic 2:1-2, 8-9).

While this problem is not as acute in our country as in some others, it nevertheless exists. In some sections of our country the acquiring of large tracts of land by wealthy individuals, institutions, and corporations has reached serious proportions. In some communities the local population has been almost completely displaced. The government encourages this kind of absentee ownership through its tax laws.

In many Latin American countries this problem is even more acute as millions of people have been reduced to a state of perpetual poverty. In Brazil, for example, two words often heard are "agrarian reform." Disappointed with the government's failure to find a solution to their problems, the masses are organizing to demand a fair share of their nation's wealth and resources. The main targets of their agitation are the *latifundiários*, the owners of the large country estates, who live in royal splendor while the laborers who cultivate their farms are kept in a state of virtual bondage. Many of these *latifundiários* oppose the preaching of the gospel among their laborers. This might place dangerous ideas in their minds. It might cause them to want to be free.

Verses 9-10 teach that such greed is self-defeating. The large mansions of the greedy land-grabbers will one day stand empty and desolate. Their fields will lose their productivity. Ten acres of vineyard will produce only one bath (about six gallons of wine). The yield of grain will be so small that the farmer will actually reap less than he sows. He will sow ten bushels (a homer) and gather only one bushel (an ephah).

History witnesses to the truth of this prophecy. In country after country, as social change and revolution have come, the first persons to be affected have often been the large landowners and the rich.

Woe to the intoxicated carousers (5:11-17). This woe is addressed to Judah's heavy drinkers. They are described as those whose parties are nothing but occasions for getting drunk to music. They begin early in the morning and continue until late at night until their minds are inflamed with wine.

In their drunken stupor they are unaware that God is at work in their day. "They do not regard the deeds of the Lord, or see the work of his hands." This may refer to the inevitable retribution that will fall upon their heads, or it may refer to the downfall of their nation, which is already ripe for destruction.

In verses 14-17, Sheol, the realm of the dead, which was thought to lie under the surface of the earth, is pictured as a gaping monster. It is waiting to swallow the proud city and its calloused throngs. After this has occurred, flocks of sheep will graze among the ruins of the once proud city.

When the prophet speaks of the holy God's showing himself holy (v. 16), he means simply that God will exhibit his character as God. God is holy, and it is this that distinguishes him from man. He now proposes to reveal his character to men in his mighty acts of judgment.

Woe to those who toil at sin and mock at God (vv. 18-19). These are harnessed to their sin. They draw it after them as oxen draw the cart to which they are harnessed.

At the same time they defiantly challenge God to judge them. They neither believe that he can or will. This is practical atheism, the denial that God is at work in his creation. This was one of the problems that Malachi had to face in his day (cf. Mal 2:17; 3:13-15).

Woe to those who are incapable of making moral distinctions (v. 20). How forcefully this word speaks to our age with its moral relativity and its situational ethic! Pity the Christian who can no longer distinguish between good and evil, between light and dark, between sweet and bitter! Life for this person has become confused, obscure, and insipid.

Woe to the self-appointed wise men (v. 21). These are Israel's self-made men. They are ever learning but never coming to a knowledge of the truth.

Woe to those skilled at mixing wine and perverting justice (vv. 22-25). These were Israel's men of distinction, her heroes of the wine cups. They were men who knew how to hold their liquor.

They also knew how to pull a fast deal by greasing the palms of the officials and judges. Their fate, and that of all those charged in this series of woes, was already sealed. They would burn up and blow away (v. 24). Their day of punishment would be a day of untold agony and horror (v. 25).

The greatest mistake we could make in our study of Isaiah would be to regard his messages as having been addressed only to people who lived long ago. We also need to pay attention to what he said, for we are more like the people of Judah than we care to admit. Isaiah's messages are addressed to us also and we must study them to see what God has to say to us. We have not really understood the words of Scripture unless we become existentially involved in them. Speak, Lord, for thy servants are listening!

Chapter Four

ISAIAH AND THE SYRO-EPHRAIMITIC CRISIS
7:1–8:15

This passage must be understood against the background of Assyria's threat to the existence of the small countries surrounding Judah. The date was around 735–734 B.C., when the Assyrian Empire was at the height of its power. It threatened to swallow up all of the small Mediterranean nations.

In order to protect themselves, certain of these nations decided to form a coalition. In unity there would be greater security. The two leading parties in the coalition were Rezin of Damascus (Syria) and Pekah of Samaria (Israel).

Ahaz came to the throne in Judah in 735 B.C. According to 2 Kings 16:2, he was only twenty years of age at this time. Pressure was exerted to force him to join the coalition against Assyria. When he refused, Pekah and Rezin attacked him. Because of his youth and inexperience, Ahaz was filled with terror at the presence of invading troops on his soil. Panic-stricken, he resorted to the extreme measure of offering one of his sons as a burnt offering (2 Kgs 16:3), thereby hoping to avert the wrath of God.

The Sign of Shear-jashub (7:1-9)

It was in the midst of these momentous events that Ahaz had his encounter with Isaiah. Possibly just before the siege of Jerusalem began, Ahaz went out to inspect the city's water supply. The "conduit of the upper pool" (v. 3) probably refers to an open trench leading from the Gihon spring to a reservoir. This was before Hezekiah had dug a tunnel to bring waters of this spring to a reservoir inside the walls of Jerusalem.

Since Gihon seems to have been associated with the coronation of kings (cf. 1 Kgs 1:33-34), Isaiah's appearance there would have carried added significance. This was a crucial moment for Judah. God had indeed promised that David would never lack a son to sit upon his throne (2 Sam 7:16; cf. Ps 132:11-12), but the very existence of the Davidic dynasty was now being threatened. It was the purpose of Pekah and Rezin to dethrone Ahaz and to replace him by the son of Tabeel (v. 6), an otherwise unknown person whose name probably meant "good-for-nothing."

As Isaiah went out to meet Ahaz he was accompanied by his little son Shear-jashub. His name signified "a remnant shall return." This could be interpreted as either threat or promise. His presence on this occasion was probably intended as a warning to Ahaz. If he did not trust the Lord in this crisis, his land would pass through troubled times and only a remnant of his people would survive.

When Isaiah met Ahaz he attempted to persuade him to trust God alone for deliverance in this crisis (v. 4). Isaiah's advice was good religion and it was good politics. It was good religion because the appropriate response to the crisis was faith, not feverish activity and anxiety over the defenses of Jerusalem.

Isaiah's advice was also based on a sound appraisal of the political situation. So certain was he that the Syro-Ephraimitic alliance would fail that he referred to Pekah and Rezin as "these two smoldering stumps of firebrands." Firebrands smolder and smoke most when they are going out.

Nothing is said in this oracle concerning the king's response to Isaiah's exhortation to faith and quiet trust in the Lord. We are informed, however, that he resolved to appeal directly to Tiglath-pileser, the king of Assyria, to come to his aid (2 Kgs 16). He emptied the Temple and court treasuries in order to pay for this assistance. In the light of Isaiah's stand on the matter of faith, we may be sure that he regarded Ahaz's appeal to Tiglath-pileser as synonymous with arrogance, unbelief, and contempt for God. It was equivalent to setting the power of man above the power of God. Ahaz had already settled on his course of action and he probably greeted Isaiah's exhorta___ with stony silence.

To Isaiah, more than to any other Old Testament prophet, belongs the credit for having coined the concept of faith. Isaiah taught that a new era had arrived, an era in which only the community of the faithful could claim to be in covenant relationship with God.

A similar call to faith is in 28:14-22. It was addressed to those who had taken refuge in their clever political alliances. The things in which these leaders trusted would be swept away and a new order established in which only those who had faith would stand the test. These exhortations of Isaiah point to a new people of God, a people whose only continuity is faith.

Isaiah's appeal to Ahaz was underscored by a play on words: "If you faith is not sure, your throne will not be secure" (cf. v. 9). For a remarkably similar play on words, see 2 Chronicles 20:20: "Believe in the Lord your God, and you will be established; believe his prophets, and you will succeed." To Isaiah there was only one alternative to frustration, defeat, and death, and that was absolute faith in God.

It should be said, however, that Isaiah was no pacifist, nor did he make light of human effort. He never condemned human effort in itself, but rather the attitude in which human effort was undertaken. He taught that a nation's true safety lay not in reliance upon human efforts but upon God (cf. 26:3-4; 30:15-16; 32:17).

The Sign of Immanuel (7:10-17)

There is every indication that these verses describe events that took place subsequent to those in verses 1-9. How much later is a matter of speculation. Perhaps it was before Ahaz had actually sent his appeal to Tiglath-pileser.

To the skeptical Ahaz, the prophet offers a sign. The word "sign" is used seventy-nine times in the Old Testament, twenty-five of which relate to the plagues of Egypt. A sign has been defined as anything in nature or history that appears wonderful, mysterious, surprising, astonishing, or awe inspiring.

In the Old Testament a sign never stands by itself but is always closely linked with the word of God. Its purpose is to confirm the word of God spoken through one of his messengers. A good example of this was Moses' use of signs to convince Pharaoh that God had commanded him to deliver the Israelites. Signs were given to impress the skeptical and to make believers out of scoffers.

Ahaz refused to ask a sign. He knew that if he did so he would have to abandon his own course of action. He pretended that his refusal was based on religious conviction: he would not tempt the Lord! The truth of the matter was that he resented the prophet's meddling in political affairs. Religion had its place in life, he thought, but this was far removed from the sphere of politics.

The sign would be given in spite of Ahaz's refusal to request it. The sign was to be the birth of a child whose name would be called Immanuel, translated "God with us." The literal rendering of verse 14 would be:

> Therefore the Lord himself will give you a sign; behold the young woman, pregnant and bringing forth a son, and she shall call his name Immanuel.

One hardly knows where to begin in seeking answers to the questions posed by this passage. Who was the young woman to whom Isaiah referred? Was she the king's wife? Was she the prophet's wife? Was she some other woman known to both king and prophet who was pregnant and about to give birth to a child? Was the promise of the sign given unconditionally, or was it predicated upon Ahaz's acceptance of it in faith? Was the sign fulfilled in the lifetime of Isaiah? If so, who then was this child called Immanuel? Why does the Septuagint translate the Hebrew word for "young woman" by the Greek word for "virgin"? How are we to interpret Matthew's use of the Septuagint translation of Isaiah 7:14 as a prophecy of the birth of Christ?

The word rendered "a young woman" comes from a root meaning to be ripe. It describes a young woman who is sexually mature and, therefore, capable of entering into marriage. The word is neutral with regard to the question of virginity.

It should be noted that this child was to serve as a sign to Ahaz. His birth was a sign to Ahaz of the certain fulfillment of the word of the Lord concerning Pekah and Rezin (v. 16).

Elsewhere in Isaiah whenever a person serves as a sign it is because of the symbolic name he bears (cf. 8:18). This was true of Shear-jashub and Maher-shalal-hash-baz. The same could be said of the children of Hosea. Likewise the child in Isaiah 7:14 served as a sign because of the significance of his name. Actually the child's timely birth, his name, and his early childhood were symbolic of a whole sequence of events prophesied in 7:14-17 and expanded in 7:18-25.

Attention has been called to the similar use of the word "sign" in Exodus 3:12. When Moses asked for a sign, God's answer to him was almost identical to that which Isaiah gave Ahaz. "But I will be with you; and this shall be a sign for you, that I have sent you." The period belongs here. The additional statement about serving God on this mountain is not the sign. The sign is "I will be with you."

The sign, therefore, is the sign of Immanuel, the assurance of God's abiding presence with his people. This is the only promise God ever makes to his servants. They are not promised success, riches, popularity, or an easy life. The only assurance they have is the assurance that if they are obedient to God's will they will never walk alone (cf. Matt 28:19-20).

The significance of the birth of a child must not be overlooked. There are three pivotal points in the history of God and his people in the Old Testament. They are the beginning of the patriarchal period (Gen 12), the beginning of the nation's history at the exodus (Exod 1), and the beginning of the monarchy (1 Sam 1). Each of these sections begins with an extended account of the birth of a child. In Genesis, it is Isaac; in Exodus, Moses; and in 1 Samuel, Samuel. The New Testament also begins with the birth narratives of John the Baptist and of Jesus. God's mighty acts in history always begin with the birth of a child.

The sign of Immanuel is a message of hope and ultimate victory. The time of victory, however, is preceded by a time of affliction. The land will be reduced to a pastoral state as the Assyrians sweep through it (v. 17). The reference to the child's eating curds and honey (v. 15)

may mean that while still a child his life will be in jeopardy, and he
will have to flee to the wilderness. Before the child reaches the age of
moral responsibility, perhaps to be understood as twelve years of age,
the two kings threatening Ahaz will be put to flight (v. 16). This
prophecy was strikingly fulfilled when Tiglath-pileser overran Israel
about 733 B.C. (cf. 2 Kgs 15:29-30) and in 732 destroyed Damascus.

Since the birth of Immanuel was to be a sign to Ahaz of the imminent defeat of the two kings who were attacking him, we are left
with the thorny problem of deciding who Immanuel was. Since the
word translated "a young woman" bears the definite article, the most
natural explanation is that she was the queen and that her son was a
royal child. The traditional Jewish interpretation is that the child
whose birth is predicted was Hezekiah. There is further evidence that
the child would be born to Ahaz and to his queen in the Septuagint's
rendering of verse 12. "She shall call his name" is altered to read "and
you [masculine] shall call his name."

If this interpretation is correct, then this is a messianic prophecy
and should be linked with similar prophecies in Isaiah 9:1-7; 11:1-9;
Micah 5:2-6; and Zechariah 9:9-10. Isaiah, in recognizing the faith-
lessness of the king of Judah, pointed beyond the coming destruction
to a time when God would begin again and raise up a worthy heir to
the throne of David.

It is obvious that Isaiah expected this to take place during his own
lifetime. He had no way of knowing that the fulfillment of this hope
would be delayed for several centuries. In the fullness of time this
prophecy was transposed to a higher key and the messianic reign predicted by the prophets was inaugurated at the birth of Jesus. God was
with us in the person of his Son.

The Dire Consequences of the Policy of Ahaz (7:18-25)

Ahaz regarded the advice of Isaiah as mere fanaticism. Instead of
accepting it, he sent messengers to the king of Assyria with all the
silver and gold that could be found in the Temple and palace treasuries (2 Kgs 16:5-9). He bade the messengers say to the king of Assyria,
"I am your servant and your son. Come up, and rescue me from the

hand of the king of Syria and from the hand of the king of Israel, who are attacking me." Ahaz received help, but it cost Judah her independence, both political and religious (cf. 2 Kgs 16:10-20).

Verses 18-25 are threats uttered against Judah. They describe the outcome of Ahaz's stupidity in the handling of his foreign policy.

There are four brief messages in this section, each introduced by the words "in that day." They carry forward the thought of verse 17 and belong to the same period in Judah's history.

The first oracle (vv. 18-19) predicts that Ahaz's policy will convert Judah into a battleground, with the armies of Egypt and Assyria converging upon her. The second oracle (v. 20) predicts in highly symbolic language that the land will be devastated by the Assyrians. The next two oracles (vv. 20-22, 23-25) describe the effects of the invasion upon the people and the land. The people who survive the invasion will be reduced to a life of utter simplicity, living like desert nomads. The land will revert to thickets of briers and thorns, fit only for hunting or for the grazing of stray cattle and sheep.

The Sign of Maher-shalal-hash-baz (8:1-4)

This oracle also comes from the time of the Syro-Ephraimitic crisis and is closely related to 7:1-17. Once again the prophet foretells the imminent downfall of Syria and Israel and predicts that the instrument of their destruction will be the Assyrians.

The prophet's message was attested in an unusual manner. He took a large tablet and in the presence of reliable witnesses wrote on it this cryptic message: "To Maher-shalal-hash-baz." This should be translated "the spoil speeds, the prey hastens." It was a message of doom for Syria and Israel and a message of encouragement to Judah and the house of Ahaz.

The prophet then went in to his wife and she conceived and bore a son. The son was named Maher-shalal-hash-baz. His birth, like that of Immanuel, was to serve as a sign of the imminent destruction of Syria and Israel. Before he was old enough to say the most simple words, such as daddy and mother, the two lands menacing Judah would be captured and plundered by the king of Assyria (v. 4).

The similarities between this passage and the Immanuel passage
(7:10-17) are remarkable. In both a message is addressed to the people
of Judah, particularly to the ruling house. In both, the birth of a child
and his unusual name serve as a sign of God's presence with his people
and of the imminent overthrow of their enemies. Both are designed to
cause Ahaz and his people to trust God in the current crisis and not to
take matters into their own hands. In each case, however, the appeal to
faith is rejected. No matter how earnestly the prophet pleaded with his
people, they were determined to follow their own counsel.

The Oracle of the Two Rivers (8:5-8)

After Isaiah's second failure to persuade Ahaz to pursue a policy based
on faith, he pronounced a prophecy of judgment on his unbelief. He
uses a vivid figure of speech to describe the Israelites' rejection of
God's offer of assistance. They have refused the waters of Shiloh that
flow gently. Shioh has been identified as a small aqueduct or trench
that carried water from the spring of Gihon to a pool inside the city
walls. This gentle stream was to Isaiah a symbol of quiet confidence
in God.

The Israelites had rejected the path of faith and had taken counsel
of their fears. Therefore, the waters of a mighty river, even the king of
Assyria, would sweep over their land. Verse 8 seems to indicate that
this was to occur during the reign of Immanuel.

An Affirmation of Faith (8:9-10)

This oracle is addressed to the "peoples" and "far countries." This presumably included Syria and Israel, as well as any other nation that
might conspire against God's chosen people. In the end their cleverly
devised plots would backfire and they themselves would be the vic-
tims.

The closing words of this oracle have a significance that is
obscured in the translation into English. The Hebrew reads: "Take
counsel together, but it will come to nought; speak a word, but it will
not stand, *because of Immanuel,*" This oracle then belongs with the

Immanuel oracle in 7:10-17. In both places the sign of Immanuel is the sign of hope and of ultimate victory. Isaiah believed that God was firmly in control of history. Even when he elected to judge his people he did not relinquish his control over them.

The Fear of God and the Fear of Man (8:11-15)

This closing oracle is also related to the Syro-Ephraimitic crisis. In it God addresses a word of warning to the prophet. There is evidence that in those panic-filled days even he needed to have his faith strengthened.

God spoke to the prophet "with a strong hand," that is, he admonished him sharply. He commanded him to stand against the tide of public opinion and not to be swept off his feet in this crisis. He was to fear God, and then he would have no cause to fear man.

God is described in verse 14 as "a sanctuary" and as "a stone of offense" or "a rock of stumbling." To those who fear him he is a sanctuary. But to those who fear the wrath of men he is a stone of offense, a rock of stumbling, a trap, a snare.

I heard a sermon once on the subject of fear. The speaker stated that when persons fear God they love one another. When they cease to fear God, however, they begin to fear one another. Then the sinner begins to fear himself, so that fear becomes an obsession, and psychology replaces religion. The depth of despair is reached when those who no longer fear God are afraid of the tiniest thing in God's universe, even the atom. This is an apt commentary on modern man's spiritual condition.

Chapter Five

ORACLES OF BLESSING AND JUDGMENT

8:21–12:6

Light Shines in the Darkness (8:21–9:7)

This oracle belongs to the period from 732 to 722 B.C. It describes the consternation of the people of Zebulun and Naphtali when they were conquered by the Assyrians. Zebulun and Naphtali were two of the northernmost tribes of Israel. They were apparently occupied by Tiglath-pileser during the Syro-Ephraimitic crisis.

This oracle also looks forward to the time when the Assyrians will be driven out and a messianic king installed in Judah. This will occur as one magnificent act of the Lord.

In 8:21-22 there is a somber picture of the few survivors of the Assyrian invasion. As they wander through their devastated land in a fruitless search for food, they angrily curse their king, who has led them into this plight, and their God, who has seemingly abandoned them. Wherever they look they see only unrelieved darkness; there is no ray of light.

Suddenly the picture changes. The time of anguish gives way to a time of rejoicing (9:1). The people of Zebulun and Naphtali break forth into a hymn of thanksgiving to God for the salvation he has wrought. The contrast between 8:22 and 9:2 reminds one of the first light of creation that broke upon the primeval darkness and chaos. Those who had walked in darkness now saw a great light (v. 2).

The joy of the people was like the joy of the harvest, or like the joy of warriors dividing the spoil after a victory on the field of battle (v. 3). There are two reasons for their rejoicing. The first is that their oppressors have been defeated and their servitude has ended (v. 4). The second reason is that war has been abolished and the age of peace has begun (v. 5). The oppressor's armament, which lies abandoned on the battlefield, will be gathered and burned.

And why has this sudden change come about? It is because a child has been born (v. 6)? The verbs in this section are almost all perfects. So certain is the prophet that these events will occur that he describes them as if they had already occurred. The battle is the Lord's and its outcome does not depend upon human resources.

What is so unusual about this child? In the first place, he fulfills a unique mission. The government rests upon his shoulders, and he rules in justice and in righteousness. In other words, he is the long-awaited messiah, the son of David. In him is realized the ideal of a righteous and just reign over the house of Israel.

In the second place, he is unique because of the names given to him. Just as ancient kings and pharaohs were given exalted titles on the occasion of their succession to the throne, so this child is given a series of throne names.

He is called Wonderful Counselor, literally "a wonder of a counselor." This implies that his counsel comes from God alone.

He is called Mighty God, literally "God of a hero." This is the most crucial title in the entire list. It has been translated as "Divine Warrior." Does this name ascribe divinity to the child-king, or is it merely an exalted title given to the divinely endowed king? The latter interpretation is probably correct. But while the title does not ascribe divinity to the child-king, it does teach that the qualities he possessed were present in a wonderful, superhuman degree. In other words, he was divinely endowed with wisdom, with might, with a fatherly spirit, and with concern for the welfare of his subjects.

He is called Everlasting Father, literally "father of eternity." And he is called "Prince of Peace." The word "peace" means much more than the cessation of hostilities. It describes the rich, harmonious, joyful, and creative life of God's redeemed.

Who was this child so divinely endowed? The traditional Jewish interpretation is that he was Hezekiah, the son of Ahaz. But while the prophet may have wished that Hezekiah would be a wonderful counselor and a prince of peace, he was this only in a very limited sense. The hopes of the prophet were fully realized only in the birth of Jesus, who is called both Christ (Messiah) and King of the Jews.

God's Fruitless Chastisement of Israel and Its Lesson for Judah (9:8–10:4)

God has chastised Israel but she has refused correction (9:8-21). This oracle directed against the Northern Kingdom is arranged in three strophes (8-12, 13-17, 18-21). Each ends with the same refrain: "For all this his anger is not turned away and his hand is stretched out still." This passage has been referred to as "the refrain song." The same refrain appears in 5:25 and 10:4. The stretched-out arm of God is a symbol of wrath and judgment (cf. Exod 6:6; Isa 23:11; Ezek 6:14).

The word referred to in verse 8 is the prophetic word of judgment. It will come crashing down upon Israel. The word spoken by the prophet has power to break down and to destroy (cf. Jer 1:9-10; Zech 5:1-4; Heb 4:12-13). The word of God will not return unto him void (empty) but will accomplish his purpose for it (Isa 55:10-11).

God has chastened Israel in vain, for a succession of disasters has left her still proud and self-sufficient (vv. 9-12). No matter how severely God punishes her, Israel will not receive correction (vv. 13-17).

The third strophe (vv. 18-21) pictures the destructive power of evil in the life of the Northern Kingdom. Wild disorder prevails throughout the land. From the death of Jeroboam II in 746 B.C. until the fall of Samaria in 722 B.C., Israel had no fewer than six kings. Only one of these died a natural death. This period of chaos has been described as a time when one nobody after another seized the throne without even the pretense of legitimacy.

Let the wicked in Judah take warning (10:1-4). The reference to "my people" (v. 2) indicates that the prophet is addressing the unjust judges in Judah. They have issued decrees designed to deprive the poor of their rights. The prophet directs three questions to these who have gotten rich at the expense of widows and orphans (v. 3). Then without waiting for a reply he answers his own questions (v. 4). There will be no place to hide from the wrath of God.

The conclusion to this passage is found in 5:25-30. Israel's sins have provoked stroke after stroke, but the worst is yet to come. The final blow is to be the invasion and destruction of the Northern Kingdom by the Assyrians. The Lord whistles for the Assyrian army and it leaps on Israel like a lion on its prey. This prophecy was fulfilled in 722 B.C. when Samaria was destroyed.

Assyria as the Rod of God's Anger (10:5-34)

The severest crisis of Isaiah's ministry was in 701 B.C. Sargon of Assyria had died in 705 B.C. and a spirit of revolution had spread through the Assyrian Empire. In that fateful hour Isaiah had counseled a course of neutrality and trust in the Lord, as he had earlier done in the Syro-Ephraimitic crisis. Most of the oracles in chapters 28–33 belong to this period (cf. 30:1-15; 31:1-3).

Isaiah's advice was ignored once more (cf. 28:7-13; 29:7-22; 30:16). The inevitable followed. Assyria's new king, Sennacherib, proved to be master of the situation. He put down revolts in Babylon and then marched westward. One of his armies defeated the Egyptians and another moved across Samaria.

Isaiah 10:28-31 gives a vivid account of the rapid advance of this latter army. According to Sennacherib's own records he ravaged forty-six of Hezekiah's walled cities and laid siege to Jerusalem. He claimed that "like a caged bird I shut up Hezekiah in Jerusalem, his royal city."

Isaiah 1:4-9 describes the devastated state of Judah and Jerusalem. Sennacherib demanded tribute from Hezekiah (cf. 2 Kgs 18:14-16), as well as the surrender of Jerusalem. The history of these events and of the unexpected delivery of Jerusalem is contained in 2 Kings 18–19 (cf. Isa 36-37).

In this crisis Isaiah counseled Hezekiah to refuse the demands of the enemy (cf. 37:33-35; 31:4-9; 29:1-8; 30:27-33). The prophet was vindicated when the Assyrian army was overrun by a plague and had to withdraw (cf. 2 Kgs 19:35). It is possible that Isaiah 22:1-14 comes from this time. If so, it describes the victory celebrations within

Jerusalem. In the midst of the rejoicing the prophet stands alone, weeping for "the destruction of the daughter of my people."

Chapter 10 belongs to this period. Here Isaiah gives classic expression to his faith that God is directing all history in accordance with his purpose of establishing his kingdom on earth. Although the Assyrian seems invincible, it is God and not the Assyrian who is the sovereign ruler of history.

The proud Assyrian is nothing more than a rod in God's hand. When God has finished chastening Judah he will break the rod and cast it away. The people of the Bible knew that no matter how much rope the tyrants had, the end of the rope was in the hands of God.

This chapter opens and closes with God firmly in control of history. Scholars have referred to this chapter as an affirmation of Isaiah's philosophy of history. His philosophy is very simple. History is "his-story," the story of God's acts in history to carry out his purpose for his people and for all mankind.

The Messianic Age (11:1-16)

This passage describes the reign of the ideal king (vv. 1-9) and the future restoration of Israel (vv. 10-16).

This is one of the most exalted portrayals of Messiah in the Old Testament. He will sprout from the stump of Jesse when the present ruling house of David has been destroyed. He is the remnant of the house of David.

He is endowed with the spirit of the Lord. Six specific gifts of the spirit are mentioned (cf. Gal 5:22-23). The first two stress his wisdom; the second pair, his administrative ability; and the third pair, his piety.

Messiah will be the perfect judge of his people (vv. 3-5). He will not judge by outward appearances, but will deliver the needy and destroy the godless.

The conditions that will prevail in Messiah's reign are described in verses 6-9. Animals and people will live together in a paradise-like relationship. No living creature will injure or destroy another living creature. "They shall not hurt or destroy in all my holy mountain." Nature, now subject to corruption because of man's sin, is destined to share at long last in the redemption of God's people. This will occur when "the earth shall be full of the knowledge of the Lord as the waters cover the sea" (v. 9).

The word "root" in verse 10 is a technical term for Messiah. The same word occurs in 53:2, "a root out of dry ground" (cf. also Rev 22:16). Here Messiah stands like a flagstaff around which the nations rally. When he reigns, the outcasts of Israel and Judah also will be gathered from the four corners of the earth (v. 12). Ephraim, another name for Israel, and Judah will be reconciled (v. 13). There will be a highway for the returning exiles, as there was in the day when Israel came out of Egypt (vv. 15-16).

A Song of Thanksgiving (12:1-6)

When Israel came out of Egypt, she sang a hymn of praise to God for his mighty deliverance (Exod 15:1-18). Now the prospect of a greater deliverance calls for a new song. This hymn of praise forms a fitting conclusion to this section of Isaiah's prophecies.

The first part of the hymn (vv. 1-2) pictures Israel as she praises God for his mighty deliverance. In form this resembles the psalms of individual thanksgiving (cf. Ps 116). The last part of verse 2 is a repetition of Exodus 15:2.

The second part of the hymn (vv. 3-6) begins with the metaphor of the wells of salvation, a metaphor that had special meaning for those whose life was so dependent upon wells.

Drawing water with joy from these wells meant sharing in the Lord's deliverance of his people. Israel praises God not only for his deliverance but also for his abiding presence in her midst (v. 6). Aren't you glad that sharing in the Lord's salvation always makes people want to sing!

Chapter Six

CALLED TO COMFORT
40:1-31

When readers leave chapter 39 of Isaiah and cross over to chapter 40, they cover a time span of almost two centuries. They are ushered from the eighth into the middle of the sixth century B.C. Assyria had long since passed from the scene. Babylon had been ruling the world for more than a half century, but was now tottering on the brink of destruction. The emerging world power was Persia, ruled over by Cyrus.

The Jews had been in captivity since 587 B.C. Jerusalem and its temple had been devastated and the surrounding countryside depopulated. The long night of captivity was about to end, however, and the first rays of the new day could be seen in the east. The prophet hailed Cyrus as God's chosen instrument for the coming liberation of his people (cf. Isa 44:26 to 45:6).

Chapters 40–55 should be dated about 540 B.C., just prior to the Jews' release from exile and their return to Palestine. The predominant literary form in this second part of the book is the eschatological hymn. In these hymns verbs in the perfect tense are often used to describe future events, as though they had already occurred (cf. 40:9-11; 42:10-13; 49:13; 52:9-10). In form and in content these hymns are closely related to the psalms.

It has been said that Isaiah contributed more than any other prophet to the development of biblical eschatology. Throughout chapters 40–66 there is an intense eschatological expectation. It was this certainty of God's triumph that enabled the prophet of the exile to live confidently and joyfully even when the powers of evil seemed to have the upper hand. It is significant that Isaiah 40:3 was on the lips of John the Baptist when he began his ministry (Matt 3:3). Both Jesus and John were strongly influenced by Isaiah.

Behold Your God! (40:1-11)

The prophet is commanded to comfort God's people (v. 1). Those who accept the view that chapters 40–66 were written by an anonymous prophet of the exile regard this section as the prophet's own account of his call and commission.

To comfort does not mean to console people in the midst of their troubles, but to assure them that their troubles will soon be over. The prophet was to console Israel through the word that he spoke. His word was not his own but God's, and therein lay its transforming power. It was an abiding word (40:8) and a creative word charged with power to effect God's purposes (55:10-11).

Israel needed to be consoled. One of the recurring themes in this prophecy is the discouragement of Israel (40:27; 41:10, 14). Israel's disillusionment during the Babylonian exile is the theme of other Old Testament passages also (cf. Ezek 37 and Ps 137).

The prophet is told to speak tenderly to Jerusalem (40:2). The literal meaning of this is, "Speak to the heart of Jerusalem." To "speak to the heart" is an idiom that occurs nine times in the Old Testament. It describes Joseph's reassuring words to his brothers in Egypt (Gen 50:21), David's words to his troops after Absalom's defeat (2 Sam 19:7), Hezekiah's words in praise of the Levites (2 Chron 30:22), and Hezekiah's words of encouragement to the besieged defenders of Jerusalem (2 Chron 32:6). These examples show that it is an expression of encouragement, of reassurance, and of renewed hope.

But it has an even richer meaning. Five of its nine occurrences describe the lover's wooing of his beloved. It is used of Shechem's wooing of Dinah (Gen 34:3), of Boaz's concern for Ruth (Ruth 2:13), of the Levite's overtures of his estranged wife (Judg 19:3), and twice of God's tender concern for his estranged people (Hos 2:14; Isa 40:2). This expression is peculiarly the language of love, a metaphor of courtship and marriage (cf. Isa 54:1-8).

The comfort offered to Israel is not the comfort of a cheap grace that glosses over the sins of the past. She is comforted because her iniquities have been pardoned and because she has received from the Lord's hand punishment in full measure (v. 2).

The voice of comfort is followed by the voice of preparation (vv. 3-5). The Lord is soon to appear in his glory, and the way must be prepared so that all flesh may see him. In the Old Testament the wilderness is sometimes used as a symbol of servitude, of discipline, and of punishment for sin (Hos 2:14). Life cut off from God is a barren wasteland. Only the return of God can restore it to its beauty and usefulness.

There is a division of opinion among scholars as to whether the highway in verse 3 is the road from Babylon to Jerusalem that is to be traveled by the returning exiles, or the way by which God himself is to return to his people. The latter suggestion seems to be more in harmony with the context. In chapter 40 there is no mention of the return of the exiles. The primary theme of this section is the glorious appearing of Israel's God.

When first commissioned, the prophet seemed reluctant to obey (v. 6). The ground and cause of his reluctance was his pessimistic view of his audience. He saw nothing enduring in them. All flesh was like grass, soon to wither and fade away (vv. 6-7).

The voice that speaks in verses 3-6 is probably that of a heavenly messenger sent to summon the prophet. After listening to the prophet's objections in verses 6-7, he responds in verse 8. He acknowledges the truth of what the prophet has said: grass *does* wither, and flowers *do* fade. But the word of our God will stand forever. Let the prophet look away from the frailty of human beings to the permanence of the word of God. Then he will never have cause to fear failure or defeat, for the word he proclaims will effect its own fulfillment (cf. 55:10-11).

A call goes out for Zion and Jerusalem to ascend a high mountain and to proclaim to all the cities of Judah the good news of God's appearing (v. 9). God is presented on the stage of world history with a threefold "behold" (vv. 9-10). Dramatic use is made of this word throughout Isaiah 40–66 (cf. 42:1; 52:13; 62:11; 65:13). It occurs fifty times in these chapters alone.

The Lord who comes is strong, but gentle (vv. 10-11). His strength is the strength of a mighty warrior-king, and his gentleness is the gentleness of a shepherd who leads and defends his flock.

The Omnipotent God (40:12-31)

Israel's God is infinite in power and in wisdom (vv. 12-14). A favorite
literary device of this prophet is the rhetorical question (vv. 12-14, 18,
21, 25, 27-28). He must have stimulated the minds of his listeners
with his probing questions.

The impotence of the nations stands in sharp contrast to the
omnipotence of God (vv. 15-17). On the basis of Ugaritic parallels,
the first half of verse 15 should be rendered, "Behold, the nations are
like a drop from a rain cloud." This must not be interpreted to mean
that God has no concern for the nations, for one of the features of this
prophecy is its universality (cf. 45:22; 49:6; 56:6-8). It means, rather,
that the nations pose no threat to God nor to his people.

Isaiah 40–66 is notable for its rich variety of literary forms. These
chapters do not present a single theme that is logically developed.
They are more like a symphony that develops one motif through
many variations. They have also been described as a great tapestry
woven from the strands of many literary forms.

One of these forms is the idol satire. A good example of this is
found in verses 18-20 (cf. 41:5-7; 44:9-20; 46:5-7). In these satires the
author shows the utter stupidity of idolatry. Both the rich and the
poor have their idols. The rich man's idol consists of a wooden core
with gold and silver overlay (v. 19). The poor man's idol is any piece of
wood that can be carved into an image (v. 20). These idol satires serve
to emphasize the uniqueness of Israel's God.

Perhaps we also need to be reminded of the stupidity of idolatry.
Even after twenty centuries of Christianity, men still turn to such stu-
pidities as yoga, astrology, palm reading, and luck charms. These
forms of idolatry can help no one.

Israel's God exercises lordship over creation and history (vv. 21-
26). He is the Creator, and all nature is under his control. The verb "to
create" is used no fewer than twenty-one times in chapters 40–66 (cf.
40:26, 28; 43:1; 45:18; 65:17). Wherever this verb appears in the Old
Testament, God is always the subject. It thus describes a unique creative act which he alone can perform.

The prophet points to the stars as a symbol of the mighty power of God (v. 26). Each evening God counts his stars, as a shepherd would count his sheep, and not one of them is missing. Some have interpreted this as a symbol of the shepherd's counting his sheep at the close of the day. Others see it as a military metaphor. God is not the shepherd of the stars but rather the commander of the hosts of heaven. He musters the stars and each stands at attention when its name is called.

When we remember that the stars were worshiped as gods, especially among the Babylonians, these words take on added meaning. The prophet is denying that the stars have any autonomy. They are all under the authority of Israel's God.

Israel's God is Lord not only of creation but also of history (vv. 23-24). He brings princes of the earth to naught, even the mighty princes of Babylon. No tyrant is safe so long as God sits upon his throne. He has but to blow upon them, and they wither and fly away.

In spite of the manifestations of God's power over creation and history, Israel has lost heart (v. 27). She complains that God is no longer concerned about her welfare. The long years of exile and foreign domination have embittered her spirit.

She complains, "My right is disregarded by my God." This reveals her legalistic way of thinking. God was under obligation to Israel, because she had perfectly fulfilled her obligations through her religious ceremonies and sacrifices. She had done her part—why did not God do his part? The prophet severely rebuked this demanding spirit. A nation as sinful as Israel was in no position to make demands upon God.

This rebuke is followed by one of the most sublime confessions of faith in all the Scriptures (vv. 28-31). The prophet tells his countrymen that their concept of God is entirely too small. They have forgotten the dimensions of the God of Israel. These words were written by one who had himself gone through the valley of despair before arriving at an unshakable faith in the sufficiency of God.

This mighty God never grows weary, and he imparts his own great strength to those who wait for him. The meaning of verse 30 is that human strength, however lusty and vigorous, will inevitably fail.

God's power is accessible to those who wait for him (v. 31). The idea of waiting for the Lord is a recurring theme in the Old Testament (Isa 49:23; 51:5; 64:4; Pss 25:3, 21; 27:14; 33:20; 37:7, 9; 40:1; 69:6). Israel is pictured throughout chapters 40–66 as the waiting community—a community now in bondage but waiting for liberation; now blind but waiting for sight; now humiliated but waiting to be exalted; now forsaken but waiting for the return of her God.

The word "to wait" is one of the most interesting words in the Bible. Its basic meaning is to wind or to twist. The word for cord in Joshua 2:18, 21 comes from this same root. To wait for God means to let him become your hope, your cord of escape, your lifeline.

This word does not mean to wait passively but to wait eagerly. Thus it is used in Psalms 56:6 and 119:95 to describe the eager expectation of evildoers who wait in ambush to slay the righteous. It is used also in Isaiah 5:4, 7 to describe the farmer's eagerness to see his crops mature. This series of pictures—the tension of the cord, the waiting in ambush, and the eager expectation of the farmer—shows the richness of this concept.

To all who wait for him, God gives new strength, different strength, his own strength. This is the meaning of the promise that those who wait for the Lord shall renew their strength. "Change" would be a better word than "renew." Those who wait on the Lord do not renew their own strength, but they exchange their strength for God's strength. Astronauts often have to change to an auxiliary power supply in mid-flight. Those who wait on the Lord switch over to a new source of power. They live not in the strength of the flesh but in the strength of the Lord.

These will then grow pinions like eagles, those high-soaring, distance-devouring kings of the air. Some have detected an anticlimax in verse 31—from flying to running and finally to walking. This is, however, an appropriate description of the life of faith. Sometimes we fly, and sometimes we run, but most of the time we walk. And the real test of faith comes not when we fly or run, but when we have to plod along. It is in the monotony of everyday life that we reveal our true character.

I recently read the account of an Indian who lived on a reservation near Juneau, Alaska. This was before the widespread use of electricity, and he had never seen an electric light. After the power lines had reached Juneau, he came into town to purchase supplies. Imagine his surprise when the shop owner pulled on a cord and the room was flooded with light.

The Indian asked to buy one of the new lights. Thinking that he had access to electricity, the merchant measured off three feet of cord, attached a socket and switch, screwed in a bulb, and handed it to him.

The Indian returned home, suspended the cord from the ceiling, and waited for darkness to fall. Then he gathered his family together, reached up and pulled on the switch—and nothing happened! Think of how disappointed he must have been. He had everything he had seen at the store, everything that was needed for light—except one thing. His cord was not connected to the source of power.

It is possible for us to be like this man. God is our true source of power, but if we are out of touch with him, his power can do us little good. If our spiritual lamps are all wired up, but not plugged in to receive his power, we will continue to live in darkness. Let us learn to wait on the Lord, so that we may experience his power in us.

Chapter Seven

GOD'S PLAN FOR HIS PEOPLE

41:1–45:13

The Advent of Cyrus and the New Exodus (41:1-20)

In this section there is further development of the theme of God's absolute authority in history. The nations who were feared by Israel, but regarded as inconsequential by God (cf. 40:15, 23), are called to an encounter with the Lord of history. The setting is that of a court-room. The nations have assembled to hear God's judgment pronounced upon them.

The nations are commanded to be silent and to renew their strength as they approach the judgment bar of God. The reference to the renewing of strength ties in with 40:31. It is probably used here in derision. God is warning them that they will need all the strength they can muster.

Once again in verses 2-4, the prophet shows his fondness for asking questions. These verses describe the victorious march of an unnamed conqueror from the east. Who is this conqueror whom victory meets at every step? Some have interpreted this as a reference to Abraham (cf. Gen 14:13-16). It is more likely that the reference is to Cyrus, who first appeared in history about 558 B.C. as the king of Anshan. He annexed Media in 550 B.C. and then proceeded to conquer Lydia (546 B.C.) and Babylon (539 B.C.). Few men's lives have influenced the course of world history as this man's life did.

Having asked who raised up this invincible conqueror, God answers his own question with a mighty word of self-revelation: "I, the Lord, the first, and with the last; I am He." The great "I am" who appeared to Moses at the burning bush (Exod 3:14) is now preparing to deliver his captive people through a second exodus.

As the news of Cyrus's victories spreads among the nations, they speed up their production of man-made gods (vv. 5-7). This is another of the prophet's satires on the futility of idolatry. All the polishing and soldering and hammering are wasted efforts, for God has chosen Cyrus to deliver his people.

The prophet returns to the theme of the discouragement of Israel in verses 8-16. The nation is first reassured by being told that her election still stands (vv. 8-10). This is at least in part an answer to the complaint voiced in 40:27. There were many in Israel who feared that the exile signified the termination of God's covenant with them. This reassurance, therefore, was needed.

We must not overlook the significance of the title that is given to Israel in verses 8 and 9. Here for the first time in the book of Isaiah she is referred to as the Lord's servant (cf. 42:1, 19; 43:10; 44:1, 2, 21, 26; 45:4; 48:20; 49:3, 5-7; 50:10; 52:13; 53:11).

This title must not be interpreted in a servile sense only, for in biblical times the "servant of the king" was a royal official. Numerous jar handles and seals have been found bearing this inscription. The servant of the king was often a trusted friend whom the king appointed to administer his affairs and to serve as his personal representative. Israel had been chosen to perform a great mission. Election and service always go hand in hand (cf. 43:10-12, 21).

The nation is further encouraged by being told that none of her enemies will prevail against her (vv. 11-16). Note the growing animosity against Israel in verses 11-12: first, feelings of hatred; second, strife; third, contentions; and, finally, open warfare.

Israel is not to fear, for her Redeemer is the Holy One of Israel (43:14). It is impossible to overemphasize the significance of the word "redeemer." This term never appears in Isaiah 1–39, but it is used a total of thirteen times in chapters 40–66 (41:14; 43:14; 44:6, 24; 47:4; 48:17; 49:7, 26; 54:5, 8; 59:20; 60:16; 63:16). The only other prophet who ever applies this term to God is Jeremiah, and he does so only once (50:34).

The verb "to redeem" is also frequently used in these chapters (cf. 43:1; 44:22, 23; 48:20; 52:3, 9; 63:9). In addition to this, the passive participle is used three times to designate Israel as the redeemed of God (51:10; 62:12; 63:4; cf. also 35:9).

The Hebrew word for redeemer is *gô'ēl.* This is a technical term drawn from family law. Its usage introduces us to a series of social customs that were peculiar to Israel. The redeemer relationship always depended upon ties of kinship. A *gô'ēl* was a near kinsman charged with certain definite responsibilities on behalf of his relative. If the relative was forced by poverty to sell himself into slavery, the *gô'ēl* was under obligation to purchase his freedom (Lev 25:47-54). If the relative was forced by poverty to sell his ancestral land, his *gô'ēl* should redeem it in order to keep it within the family or clan (Lev. 25:25). A particular kind of *gô'ēl* was the man who married the childless widow of his deceased brother in order to beget children who would continue his brother's name (cf. Gen 38:7-8; Deut 25:510; Ruth 2:20; 3:12; 4:1-12).

In addition to these responsibilities, the *gô'ēl* was under obligation to avenge the blood of his murdered kinsman (cf. Num. 35:1621; Josh 20:1-6). Blood vengeance rested on the twofold principle of the sacredness of blood (cf. Lev 17:14) and the solidarity of the tribe or family.

To refer to the Lord as Israel's Redeemer meant two things. First, it meant that the covenant bonds that bound Israel to God and God to Israel were as strong and as intimate as family ties. Second, it meant that no price was too great for God to pay for the redemption of his people (cf. 43:3-4; 54:5-8).

Israel is addressed, in 41:14, as a worm. This is either a term of endearment or an indication of the low estimate that Israel placed upon herself. It must not be interpreted as a term of abuse or of insult. The amazing announcement in this passage is that the feeble worm is going to be transformed into a mighty threshing sledge (v. 15).

Threshing sledges were sledges into whose runners iron spikes had been driven (cf. Amos 1:3). These were then weighted down with stones and dragged about over the threshing floor in order to separate the grain from the chaff.

Israel will thresh the mountains and make the hills like chaff. The mountains and hills symbolize the nations that are oppressing Israel. Soon the tables will be turned. Israel will winnow her foes and the wind will carry them away (41:16).

Israel's delivery from Babylon is described as a new exodus, far surpassing the glories of the first exodus (vv. 17-20). When Israel went out of Egypt the sea was parted and became dry land (Ex. 14:21-22). In the new exodus God will change the wilderness into a pool of water and the dry land into springs of water (v. 18).

The transformation of nature is a constant theme in chapters 40–66 (cf. 43:16-21; 48:20-21; 49:9-11; 55:12-13; 65:25). Nature is conceived of as being alive and able to respond to God's demands. Nature, now subject to corruption because of man's sin, is destined to share at last in the redemption of God's people.

God's Superiority over Idols (41:21-29)

A good title for this section would be "Impotence and Omnipotence." This again is one of the leading themes of chapters 40–66.

In verses 21-24 the prophet issues a challenge to the idol gods. They are to show that they are truly divine by three tests. (1) Can they interpret past events in such a way as to reveal their underlying significance (v. 22a)? The "former things" probably are to be interpreted as all of God's mighty acts in the history of Israel, extending from the exodus to the exile. (2) Can they predict something that is going to happen in the future (v. 23a)? (3) Can they intervene for good or ill in the course of human affairs (v. 23b)?

The challenge goes forth to the idols—and there is no reply. They have failed the test. They are nothing, and, therefore, can do nothing (v. 24). The last half of this verse implies that while God chooses Israel (cf. 41:8-9), it is the opposite with those who worship idols. Men must choose idols; idols never choose men.

At once the prophet goes on to show that God can rise to the challenge issued to the idol gods. As an example of the interpretation of past events he offers the rise of Cyrus (vv. 25-26). The idols were unable to give any word of explanation for the successes of this conqueror. Derision is heaped upon them in verse 29. They are nothing but empty wind.

The Call and Commission of God's Servant (42:1-4)

This brings us to the first of the so-called Servant Songs (42:1-4; 49:1-6; 50:4-9; 52:13–53:12). The German scholar Bernhard Duhm was the first to isolate these and to designate them "Servant Songs." In his famous commentary, published in 1892, Duhm attributed these songs to a different author from the one who wrote the rest of chapters 40–55.

There are other scholars who accept most of Duhm's conclusions but disagree with him on the question of authorship. C. R. North and H. H. Rowley, for example, believe that a second Isaiah composed these songs toward the end of his career and then inserted them into his earlier oracles. They believe this explains the differences in the description of the Servant within the songs and the Servant outside the songs.

More recent influential voices (e.g., that of James Muilenburg and James Smart) have been raised in defense of the view that these songs are an integral part of chapters 40–55. Far from marring their context, they fit naturally into the framework of the surrounding chapters. To remove them from their context does violence to them and creates far more problems than it solves.

The identity of the Servant in these songs is a much-debated subject. In several passages he is unmistakably identified as Israel (cf. 41:8; 44:1-2, 21; 45:4; 48:20; 49:3), so that the collective interpretation cannot be disregarded. On the other hand, the New Testament clearly sees the fulfillment of these prophecies in Jesus Christ (cf. Matt 8:17; 12:18-21; Acts 8:32-35; 13:47).

How are we to reconcile these two views? Perhaps we must hold them in tension and see that each has merit. When these songs were first written, they may not have been intended as prophecies of the future sufferings of Jesus. They may have referred, in the first instance, to Israel viewed as a corporate or collective personality. Israel was God's chosen Servant. In the fulfillment of her mission Israel had to endure untold suffering and persecution. Through her suffering, spiritual blessings have come to all the nations of the earth.

At the same time it must be said that the songs do not find their complete fulfillment in Israel. Neither Israel nor any individual in Israel, prior to Christ, ever measured up to the ideal of the Servant. There is a real sense in which Jesus of Nazareth was Israel, gathering up into himself all the past experiences of the nation and bringing to fulfillment her mission and destiny. The prophet did not know how perfectly his words would one day be fulfilled in the Servant who became obedient unto death, even the death of the cross. Here was perfect obedience and perfect service.

The word "behold" appears in 41:29 and again in 42:1. It serves to emphasize the contrast between the impotent idols and God's Servant. God is the speaker in 42:1-4. He calls attention to the Servant whom he has chosen and anointed (v. 1).

The sevenfold repetition of the word "not" in the Hebrew of verses 2-4 is very effective. He will not cry out; he will not lift up his voice; he will not make it heard in the streets (v. 2). The word translated "cry out" is always used of the weak crying to the strong for help. Its most common use is of the oppressed crying out to God for help (Exod 14:10; 17:4; Judg 4:3; Ps 107:6; Lam 2:18; cf. Exod 3:7; Isa 5:7). In the light of this usage, this does not mean that the Servant will be quiet and inconspicuous in the exercise of his ministry. It means, rather, that the Servant's sorrow will soon be ended and the cry of distress will be heard no more.

This same emphasis is continued in verses 3-4. The Servant will not destroy or discourage those who are striving after righteousness, however feeble they may be (v. 3). Neither will he fail or be discouraged until he has successfully finished his mission (v. 4). The nature of this mission is set forth in the threefold repetition of the word "justice." This word is usually interpreted as meaning true religion. A better interpretation would be "a just order," that is, the kind of life that will prevail on earth when all nations are brought under God's rule. This will be accomplished, according to the prophet, through the instrumentality of God's servant.

A Present Help in Time of Trouble (42:5-17)

God speaks words of encouragement to his servant people in verses 5-9. God who sends forth his Servant is the Creator of all things in heaven and on earth (v. 5). The emphasis upon the creation motif is designed to awaken faith in God. One who has revealed his power in creation is surely able to redeem his people and deliver them from their enemies.

Israel has been called to become "a covenant to the people" (v. 6). A preferable translation of this phrase would be "a confederation of peoples." This means that Israel will be the focal point for a new world order. Her mission to the nations will be that of providing light, sight, and liberty (vv. 6-7).

God is unwilling to share his glory and praise with any other god or graven image (v. 8). He is absolutely intolerant of all rivals. His superiority to all other gods is revealed in his ability to interpret the past and to predict the future (v. 9).

The word "new" is one of the key words in chapters 40–66 (cf. 41:15; 42:9-10; 43:19; 48:6; 62:2; 65:17; 66:22), though it never occurs in chapters 1–39. In using this word, the prophet is describing not the renewal of the old but the entrance of that which was previously unknown and totally unexpected. It describes all of the wonderful things that God will do on behalf of his people in the eschatological age, which the prophet believed to be near.

The "new things" wrought by God (v. 9) call for a "new song" of praise (v. 10). Even the inhabitants of the coastlands, that is, distant nations, join in praising the Lord (vv. 10, 12). This is in keeping with verses 6-7, where it is stated that God's blessings are mediated to the nations through his Servant Israel. Even the desert tribes lift up their voices and sing for joy (v. 11).

The cause for the rejoicing is that God has triumphed over his foes (v. 13). The word translated "he cries out" is a different word from that used in 42:2. It is a word drawn from the vocabulary of holy war. It describes the shout of victory that goes up on the day of battle (cf. Josh 6:10, 20; 1 Sam 17:20, 52; 2 Chron 13:15; Ezra 3:11).

God is impatient to intervene on behalf of his people (vv. 14-17). His impatience causes him to gasp and pant like a woman in labor (v. 14). This verse teaches that God's delay in redeeming his people is not due to weakness or to a lack of concern on his part. He is the sovereign Lord and he acts at the time of his own choosing.

Soon the Lord will prepare the way for his people's return to their homeland (v. 15). He will guide them as they walk in unfamiliar paths. They will neither stumble nor lose their way, for he will turn the darkness into light and make the rough places smooth (v. 16). This will happen to those who trust in him, but those who trust in graven images will be turned back and utterly put to shame (v. 17).

The Blindness and Deafness of God's Servant (45:18-25)

The reference to the blindness and deafness of God's Servant in verses 18-20 should be interpreted against the background of Isaiah 6:9-10. Israel was blind and deaf because she had obstinately refused to see and hear. In spite of her rebellion, however, she was still God's servant.

Because she had broken God's law and violated his righteousness, she had been delivered into the hands of her enemies (v. 24). Her punishment was a deliberate act on the part of God (v. 21). By allowing her to be taken into exile in Babylon he had magnified his law and made it glorious. The emphasis in this passage is upon the truth that God was firmly in control of affairs, even when his servants had to suffer humiliation and defeat (cf. 53:10). In a real sense the defeat of Israel was the vindication of God's righteousness and holiness.

The Invincible Love of Israel's Unchanging God (43:1-13)

Israel's Creator is also her Redeemer (v. 1). Two stanzas of the hymn "How Firm a Foundation" were inspired by verses 1-2:

> Fear not, I am with thee; O be not dismayed,
>   For I am thy God, and will still give thee aid;
> I'll strengthen thee, help thee, and cause thee to stand,
>   Upheld by my righteous, omnipotent hand.
> When through fiery trials thy pathway shall lie,

> My grace, all-sufficient, shall be thy supply;
> The flame shall not hurt thee; I only design
> Thy dross to consume, and thy gold to refine.

It is important to note that God does not promise a detour around waters and fire. These are inevitable parts of our earthly lot. He does promise, however, that when we pass through the waters he will be with us. O blessed promise! When given such an assurance as this, faith never asks for more. It is enough to know that God's servants never walk alone.

The language of verses 3-4 is the language of love and must not be interpreted too literally. It means that though Israel is in bondage she has a Redeemer who will pay any price, even the whole of Africa, to buy her back. There is literally nothing that God will not give in exchange for his people. This must not be interpreted to mean that other nations have no value in God's sight. Chapters 40–66 refute this position (cf. 56:6-8).

The dispersed Israelites would be gathered from the four corners of the earth (vv. 5-7). God had not forgotten them. They were called by his name and had been created for his glory (v. 7).

Israel had been called and chosen to bear witness to her incomparable God (vv. 8-13). This passage emphasizes the truth that election is always related to mission. As Israel carried out her mission of witnessing to the one universal God she would grow in knowledge, faith, and understanding (v. 10). The same could be said of God's servants in all ages. It is through our witness and service that we gain a deeper understanding of God. Faith is nurtured through service, not through idleness.

God's Deliverance and Restoration of Israel (43:14–44:5)

This section could be outlined as follows:

   a. the downfall of Babylon, 43:14-15;
   b. the new exodus, 43:16-21;
   c. unmerited grace, 43:22-28;
   d. Israel's unique relationship to God, 44:1-5.

There is value in remembering the past, and the prophet often enjoins Israel to do this (cf. 44:21; 51:1-2). There is also a real peril when we dwell too much on past experiences. The prophet, therefore, tells Israel to forget the things that are past and to direct her attention to the new thing that is about to occur (vv. 18-19a). The former things refer to the mighty acts of God performed during the exodus from Egypt (vv. 16-17). The new thing is the destruction of Babylon (v. 14) and the preservation of the exiles as they cross the desert (vv. 19-20). As God once made a path through the sea, so now he will make a way through the wilderness.

We often wonder why God chose Israel to be his servant people. A part of the answer was given above in verse 10: Israel was chosen to witness to the uniqueness of her God. A second reason is given in verse 21: Israel was chosen in order that she might declare God's praise. Israel's mission, therefore, involved witnessing and praising. Is this not also a fitting description of our mission as Christians?

Israel has not merited deliverance; but God, for his own sake, has forgiven her sins (vv. 22-28). Israel is appropriately referred to as Jacob (v. 22). Jacob, the father of the nation, was a sinner from the beginning (v. 27). Israel is reminded not only of her sinful past but also of her present failure. She does not call upon God (v. 22a). Note the use of the word "weary" in verses 22-24. There is a similar play on the word "burdened" in verses 23 and 24. The picture here is of a nation that had lost its spiritual power and vitality.

In spite of this, God both forgave and forgot all her sins and transgressions (v. 25). He did this for his own sake. This is salvation by grace alone. Some are surprised to learn that this doctrine is found not only in the New Testament but also at the very heart of the Old Testament. This is a testimony to the unity of the Scriptures.

This theme is continued in 44:1-5. As Jacob's name was once changed to Israel, so now it is changed to Jeshurun (vv. 1-2). Jeshurun means "the upright one." As elsewhere in the Bible, a changed name means a changed character. Jacob the Supplanter becomes Jeshurun the Upright One.

This change in the character of God's people will be accompanied by the outpouring of water and God's Spirit (v. 3). Both are symbols of new life and vitality (cf. Mark 1:8-10). The people so blessed will gladly acknowledge that they belong to the Lord (v. 5).

Some have identified those referred to in verse 5 as Gentiles who are converted to the Lord. They align themselves with God's chosen people by calling themselves by the name Jacob-Israel. If this interpretation is correct then a vital truth is involved here. Conversions take place when God's people are revived and anointed with his Spirit. Perhaps this explains why our witnessing is so often ineffective and unfruitful. Like Israel of old, we have lost our vitality and our power.

No God but the Lord! (44:6-23)

The names applied to him include Lord, King of Israel, Redeemer, Lord of Hosts, and Rock (vv. 6, 8). Furthermore, his sole claim to deity is expressed in the statement, "I am the first and I am the last; besides me there is no god" (v. 6). He alone is able to announce things yet to come (v. 7). Therefore, Israel has no cause to fear before the gods of the nations (v. 8).

There is a long satire against idolatry in verses 9-20. The prophet ridicules those who bow down before a block of wood (v. 19) and feed on ashes (v. 20). He describes idolatry as self-delusion (v. 20b).

It is easy for us to recognize idolatry within the non-Christian religions and yet be unaware of our own forms of idolatry. An idol is anything devised by human minds or made by human hands that becomes a substitute for God. The essence of idolatry is in setting something less than God in the place of God. Jesus did not say that no man *should* serve two masters; he said no man *could* serve two masters. We are only deluding ourselves when we try to hold on to God with one hand and to some cherished idol with the other. Idolatry within Christianity is a denial of God's claim to absolute lordship over one's life. This form of idolatry is infinitely worse than that practices among non-Christians. At the very heart of the Scriptures stands this challenge: "Choose this day whom you will serve."

Israel is admonished to remember these things and to return to her Creator and Redeemer (vv. 21-22). She is assured that she will never be forgotten by the one who created her and called her to be his

Servant. Verse 22 emphasizes the fullness of God's forgiveness. Israel's transgressions have been swept away like a morning cloud that vanishes in the heat of the day.

The thought of God's redemption causes the prophet to burst forth into a hymn of praise (v. 23). This hymn is quite similar both in form and in content to the hymns found in the book of Psalms. This brief hymn is truly a literary gem.

Cyrus as the Agent of God's Purpose (44:24–45:13)

This Persian ruler is addressed as the Lord's shepherd (44:28) and as his anointed (45:1). This latter term designates one chosen and equipped for a special task. Although it later came to be used in a technical sense as the Anointed One, or Messiah, it must not be given this meaning in the present context. In no sense could Cyrus be regarded as the Messiah. He was simply the instrument that God used to liberate his people. It is clearly stated that Cyrus did not even know God (45:4-5). God's power is such that he can use world rulers to accomplish his purposes without their knowing that they are being used.

There are really two themes that are interwoven throughout this passage: the election of Cyrus and the uniqueness of God. Here for the first time in all the Bible we meet with the definitive statement that the Lord alone is God, and that there is no other (45:5).

God's election of an individual or a community always has an underlying missionary purpose. No stronger proof of this could be found than that furnished by this passage. Even the election of Cyrus has as its purpose that men of all nations may know that besides the Lord there is no other God (45:6).

Since there is one God and only one, there is no room in this prophet's theology for even a trace of dualism. The Lord is the Creator of both light and darkness, of both weal and woe (45:7). This may mean simply that God creates light for some and darkness for others, that those who trust him live in the light, while those who oppose him walk in darkness.

On the other hand, it may be a refutation of the Persian belief that two opposing gods—Ahura Mazda, the creator of light and goodness, and Ahriman, the creator of darkness and evil—ruled the universe. In this passage both light and darkness are attributed to one beneficent Creator. The prophet believed that God was the supreme and only cause in the entire universe. His was a thorough-going monotheism that left no room for dualism.

The usual interpretation of verses 9-13 is that they are addressed to certain Jews who resented God's choice of Cyrus. The prophet reprimanded the people for questioning the purpose of God and for denying him the freedom to act as he chose. After all, he was the divine Potter, and they were only the clay in his hand (45:9). In his threefold function as Potter (45:9), Father (45:10), and Creator (45:11-12), he had the right to do as he pleased with that which belonged to him. Furthermore, he had chosen Cyrus for their benefit and not for his own (45:13).

One of the recurring themes in Isaiah 40–66 is that salvation is God's free gift. Israel is redeemed "not for price or reward" (45:13). Redemption is God's free gift. Israel does not have to earn it or deserve it. All God requires is a humble and contrite spirit (cf. 57:15).

Chapter Eight

THE CONSOLATION OF ZION

45:14–52:12

The Saviour of the World (45:14-25)

As the prophet envisions the swift victory of Cyrus and the imminent return of the Jews to their homeland, he foresees the time when God will be acknowledged as the Saviour of all nations. He believed that God's purpose included far more than just the release of a few Jewish captives and the rebuilding of the temple in Jerusalem.

What did God's purpose include? It certainly included the restoration of Israel. It also included the establishment of an order in which men of all nations would join themselves to Israel, acknowledging Israel's God as their God (v. 14). It was the establishment of God's rule among men of all nations. It included the removal of all adverse conditions that made life wretched and added to the burden of human suffering. The New Testament refers to such an order of righteousness and justice as the kingdom of God.

God's purpose in redemption included even the physical universe (vv. 18-19). God did not create the world to be a chaos, an uninhabited wasteland. He formed it to be inhabited.

These verses take us back to the Genesis account of creation. There we learn that God created the world to be good, orderly, and beautiful. Since human beings were created in the image of God, they, too, should create works of goodness, of orderliness, and of beauty. The problem is that sinful humankind creates evil instead of good, chaos instead of order, and ugliness instead of beauty.

We live in an era when human beings possess the power to destroy the earth with hydrogen bombs. Fear of the consequences has been the only deterrent to the use of such weapons. If they should ever be used, large areas of the earth would be rendered uninhabitable. This would be not only a diabolical use of power but also a violation of God's purpose in creation. He made the earth to be inhabited.

Christians should do everything within their power to remove the threat of war and to make the world a better place in which to live. When they do this, they are cooperating with God in the realization of his intention for the earth. It is his will that swords should be converted into plowshares and spears into pruninghooks.

God's purpose does not stop here. It is his desire that all the ends of the earth should look to him and be saved (v. 22). His purpose, therefore, is worldwide. How is this purpose to be achieved? One of the most important truths in this prophecy is that God works through human instrumentality to achieve his purposes. Cyrus was his instrument for the liberation of Israel. And Israel was his instrument for the conversion of the nations. And we are his witnesses and his servants in this generation. Surely, God's purpose to bring all nations to share in his salvation is worthy of our highest commitment.

This passage returns to the theme of the uniqueness of Israel's God. All who worship an idol are praying to a god that cannot save (v. 20). We are living in an age of easy tolerance when many believe that all gods are equal and that one's religion is merely a matter of personal preference. If this be true, then the prophet was wrong, and we might as well admit it. Fortunately, there are many who still believe there is only one God to whom the ends of the earth may look for salvation.

Perhaps the reason the prophet gave such stress to this truth was that the Jews were being tempted to worship the gods of Babylon. They had spent many years as exiles in this foreign land, and perhaps they had begun to feel that the gods of Babylon were superior to the God of Israel. Isaiah's answer to this attitude was a ringing affirmation of the sovereignty of God.

The prophet was confident that the purpose of God would be achieved. His confidence was based on the integrity of the word of God (v. 23). This word had gone forth from the mouth of God and would not return until every knee had bowed to him and every tongue had confessed that he was Lord (cf. Phil. 2:9-11). God had spoken and his word could never fail.

In his autobiography, Spurgeon relates the story of his conversion. He was on his way to church one Sunday morning in 1850, when a snowstorm forced him to turn into a side street and enter a little Methodist chapel. The minister did not come that morning, so a layman preached. He took as his text these words: "Look unto me, and be saved, all the ends of the earth" (45:22, KJV). His message was simple and straightforward. It spoke to the heart of the young Spurgeon. He later described his experience in these words: "An obscure child, unknown, unheard of, I listened to the Word of God; and that precious text led me to the cross of Christ. I can testify that the joy of that day was utterly indescribable."

Impotence and Omnipotence (46:1-13)

In this passage the prophet returns to the familiar theme of the folly of idolatry. The weakness of idols and the power of God are sharply contrasted. While the idols have to be carried about by men (vv. 1-2, 7), it is God who has borne his people throughout their history (vv. 3-4). The religion of idolatry is a load; true religion is a lift.

The contrast is further seen in the fact that idols are shaped by men (v. 6), while it is the mighty hand of God that truly shapes the lives and destinies of men and nations (vv. 8-11). Furthermore, if one prays to an idol, it neither answers nor saves (v. 7). In contrast to this, God is hastening the day of Zion's salvation (v. 13).

The two gods that are singled out for ridicule are Bel and Nebo (v. 1). According to ancient records, these were the two chief gods of Babylon during the sixth century B.C. Nebo is mentioned nowhere else in the Bible, but several Babylonian names compounded with Nebo occur, as, for example, Nebuchadnezzar and Abednego (Abednebo). Nebo was the son and secretary of Merodach. He was the god of writing and business, of wisdom and eloquence, of the arts and sciences.

Bel had by the sixth century B.C. become a synonym for Merodach (cf. Jer 50:2). The chief sanctuary of Merodach was at Babylon, which was sometimes referred to as the City of Merodach. Nebo's chief sanctuary was at Borsippa, located some twenty miles southwest of Babylon. These two cities were connected by a processional road along which the gods were borne by their followers, especially during the annual New Year festival.

The prophet may have had such an occasion in mind when he wrote of the idols' being carried as burdens on weary beasts. Others have suggested that he had reference to war refugees frantically trying to save their gods as the enemy advanced on Babylon. In any event he was using sarcasm to emphasize the failure of Babylon's gods.

Babylon's Day of Reckoning (47:1-15)

This chapter is a taunt song over the fall of Babylon. She is addressed as a queen who must quit her throne, strip off her robe, and perform the menial tasks of a common slave girl (vv. 1-2).

In this funeral dirge, written in the mournful *qinah* meter of 3-2 beats, the prophet indicts Babylon on four counts: her cruelty (v. 6), her false sense of security (vv. 7, 8, 10), her pride and self-adulation, and her reliance upon sorcery and astrology (vv. 12-13).

Driven from her throne, Babylon is stripped like a slave girl and shamefully exposed to her conqueror (v. 3). She suffers the loss of children and widowhood all on the same day (v. 9). Her evil is beyond atonement and no sacrifice can avert her disaster (v. 11). The fires of judgment have already been kindled, and these fires are not the kind that one sits beside in order to be warmed (v. 14). Babylon is left without anyone to save her (v. 15). Her allies wander about as helpless and as confused as she is.

Such in the end is the fate of all dictators. Babylon has committed the ultimate blasphemy of saying, "I am, and there is no one besides me," words that only God has the right to speak. It is this unbridled egotism that brings down the wrath of God upon her.

Prophecies of Rebuke and Promise (48:1-22)

Included in this chapter of extremes are words of condemnation and judgment as well as the most comforting words of divine forgiveness. The key words that give it unity are "hear," "call," "Jacob," and "name." The chapter ends with a stirring call for the exiles to depart from Babylon. This is the last reference to Cyrus and to Babylon that one encounters in the book of Isaiah.

Verses 1-11 describe the obstinate nature of God's people. Even on the eve of liberation from Babylon, even after God had shown himself to be gracious and forgiving, they were still obstinate, stiff-necked, and hardheaded (v. 4). This accounts with many other references to Israel's continuing rebellion during the exilic period (cf. 42:18-25; 43:22-24; 45:9-11; 46:8, 12). The fourfold repetition of the command to hear (vv. 1, 12, 14, 16) and the references to the nation's unwillingness to hear (vv. 18-19) make us aware that the prophet must have encountered stiff resistance from his listeners.

To be sure, the people still maintained a semblance of loyalty to God (vv. 1-2). They made their confessions and recited their creeds in a very orthodox manner. All of this, however, was mere sham, without sincerity and without justice (v. 1b). God was not fooled by their hypocrisy.

There is a contrast in these verses between "former things" (v. 3) and "new things" (v. 6). The former things have reference to the exodus from Egypt. The new things are the great events associated with Cyrus's campaigns, the liberation of Israel, and the new exodus. These new things are described as a special creation by God. God, who created the world, Israel, and the nations, also creates events. In other words, his creative power is manifested in history as well as in nature.

The only reason Israel had not been completely destroyed in the furnace of affliction was that God had deferred his anger and restrained it (vv. 9-10). He did this for his own name's sake and not because of any merit on Israel's part (v. 11). Once again the prophet emphasizes the fact that salvation is all of grace.

There is a final reference to the mission of Cyrus in verses 12-16. The last part of verse 16 is very obscure. It should be translated "And now the Lord God has sent me and his Spirit." In other words, the speaker has been endowed with the Spirit. Who is the speaker? Is it Cyrus? Is it the Servant? Or is it the prophet? The latter interpretation is probably correct, though there are advocates for all of the other positions. In any event, one should not base important conclusions on such an obscure saying.

The high cost of rebellion is the theme of verses 17-19. Israel has had the best teacher in all the world (v. 17). God not only taught them how to profit but he also led them in the way they should go. The best teacher will fail, however, if the pupil is unwilling to learn. Israel is reminded of the things she has lost by refusing to be taught (vv. 18-19). One is reminded of the words of Jesus: "O Jerusalem, Jerusalem…! How often would I have gathered your children together as a hen gathers her brood under her wings, and you would not!" (Luke 13:34).

Nothing is quite so tragic in the life of an individual or of a nation as wasted opportunity. These are still the saddest words of tongue or pen: *It might have been!* One of the key biblical words for sin is a word that means to miss the mark, to fall short of the goal. Israel's history could be described as a series of wasted opportunities. Could not the same be said of the church of our Lord Jesus Christ?

This chapter ends on a somber note. There is no peace for the wicked (cf. 57:19-21). The word "peace" is one of the key words in chapters 40–66 (cf. 48:18; 52:7; 53:5; 54:10, 13; 55:12; 57:2, 19, 21; 59:8; 60:17; 66:12). This word comes form a root that means "to be whole." It is similar in meaning to our word "health," which derives from the Anglo-Saxon word *wholth.* It signifies wholeness of being, happiness, success. It is no accident that peace and righteousness are linked together in verse 18. It is impossible to have one without the other.

The Mission of the Servant and the Glorification of Israel
(49:9–50:3)

The second of the Servant Songs is found in 49:1-6. In this passage the Servant himself is the speaker. He describes his predestination for his task (v. 1), the weapons of his warfare (v. 2a), his concealment until the proper time (v. 2b), his initial discouragement (v. 4), and the enlargement of his mission to include not only the tribes of Jacob but also all the nations of the earth (vv. 5-6).

Verse 3 has baffled interpreters. Here Israel is unmistakably designated as the Lord's Servant. And yet, according to verse 6, the Servant is sent to restore the preserved of Israel. If Israel was the Servant, how could Israel bring Israel back to God?

Various solutions have been proposed. Some would delete the word "Israel" from verse 3, although there is no textual support for doing so. Others regard the Servant as an individual who through his faithfulness had become the true representative of Israel. Another interpretation is that the Servant is the nation Israel viewed as a corporate or collective personality. Her restoration to God was to be effected as she became a witness to the ends of the earth. By losing her life in service she would truly live again. Only as she gave herself as a light to the nations would Israel once again be truly Israel. It must be admitted, however, that verses 5 and 6 constitute a serious obstacle to the collective view of the Servant. Nowhere is the tension between the individual interpretation and the collective interpretation greater than in this passage.

The momentary discouragement of the Servant (v. 4) should be compared with the complaint of Israel recorded in 40:27. Israel complained, "My right is disregarded by my God." The Servant affirmed, "Surely my right is with the Lord." It is significant that God's response to the Servant's discouragement was to enlarge his mission and to increase his responsibility. God knows that the best cure for despondence is work. One of the reasons we so often have a defeatist attitude is that we have not found a task that challenges us to give our best.

Verse 7 describes the homage that kings will pay to Israel once God's salvation has reached to the ends of the earth. This will be in sharp contrast to Israel's present status as one "deeply despised, abhorred by the nations, the servant of rulers." The theme of the homage of kings is continued in verses 22-23. Some have objected to the idea that kings and queens would become the caretakers of Israel's children and would bow down to the ground and lick the dust of Israel's feet (v. 23).

Two things need to be said in response to this objection. First, this is poetic language and therefore highly figurative. Second, the homage of kings is a spontaneous act of gratitude on their part. They render homage to Israel not because they are forced to do so but because they want to do so. It is an expression of their gratitude to the God of Israel for his wonderful salvation.

There is a renewed promise of the release from captivity in verses 8-12. Israel's children had finally come to the "time of favor," the "day of salvation" (v. 8). As they left their prisons and headed back across the desert to the land of Israel, they would experience no hardship, for God himself would accompany them (v. 10). He would lead them as a shepherd leads his flock, guiding them to green pastures (v. 9) and to springs of water (v. 10; cf. 40:11).

The wonder of it all caused the prophet to burst forth into a hymn of praise (v. 13; cf. 42:10-12; 52:9; 55:12-13). This is another of the literary gems that adorn this prophecy.

In spite of the prospect of imminent salvation, Zion was still despondent (v. 14). She felt that God has cast her off and forgotten her. There follows one of the tenderest assurances of God's unfailing love for his people that can be found anywhere in the Scriptures (vv. 15-16). A mother would forget her infant child sooner than God would forget his people. Certainly a mother's love is the strongest form of love known in the human family, but God's love is infinitely greater. He never forgets his own.

The prophet predicts that Zion will be rebuilt (v. 17) and that the new city will be too small for the new generation that will be born. Imagine urban renewal and a population explosion in the sixth century B.C.! Zion, so long bereft of her children, is suddenly thrust into the situation of the "old woman who lived in a shoe." She can only cry out in amazement and joy, "Where did all these come from?"

The question raised in verse 15 concerns God's love. Does he care? The question raised in verse 24 concerns his power. Assuming that he does care, is he able to rescue his people from their mighty conquerors? The answer to this question is given in no uncertain terms (vv. 25-26).

Are not these the same questions that we raise when we encounter perplexing problems and difficulties? Does God care? Is he able? Faith answers both of these questions with an unconditional Yes!

God's relationship to Israel is described under the figure of marriage (50:1-3). Because of Israel's sin there has been a separation, but no divorce (v. 1). God would have acted long ago to heal the breach and to end the separation had it not been for Israel's continued deafness to his call (v. 2a). His failure to redeem his people was not due, therefore, to any lack of power on his part but to their reluctance to return to him (vv. 2-3).

Israel's Triumph over Her Adversaries (50:4–51:8)

Verses 4-9 have been described as the third Servant Song, even though the term "Servant" does not appear in these verses. They are written in the first person and some have identified the speaker as the prophet himself. It is more likely, however, that the speaker is the same as in 49:1-6.

These verses describe the discipleship of the Servant (vv. 4-5), the persecution of the Servant (v. 6), the perseverance of the Servant (v. 7), and the triumph of the Servant (vv. 8-9). The fourfold repetition of "the Lord God" (vv. 4, 5, 7, 9) serves to emphasize the fact that the Servant's help comes from God alone. The verb "to help" is one of the most frequently used verbs in this prophecy (cf. 41:10, 13, 14; 44:2; 49:8; 50:7, 9). It means far more than merely to render assistance or to give first aid. It means to do everything that needs to be done on behalf of someone who is in great distress. To say that God helps is the equivalent of saying that he saves.

The Servant is assured that all his adversaries will wear out like a garment and be eaten up as by a moth (v. 9). This assurance of ultimate triumph is repeated in 51:7-8. The frightened exiles needed to be reminded that the tables would soon be turned on their oppressors and these would speedily disappear.

The contrast between the faithful Servant and his godless foes is brought to a climax in verses 10-11. The Servant walks in darkness with no light, yet he trusts in the name of the Lord and relies upon his God. His pathway, therefore, is illuminated by faith. The godless, on the other hand, kindle fires to their idols and walk in the light of these fires. At the end of their pathway there is torment and destruction. The prophet knew that Israel had to choose between these two alternatives. She must either walk in the light of faith or perish in the fire of judgment. The same two alternatives face us even today.

There are three stanzas in 51:1-8. Each begins with the command to hearken or to listen (vv. 1-3, 4-6, 7-8). The same refrain occurs at the conclusion of the last two stanzas. This wonderful poem is designed to awaken faith in the certainty and permanence of the coming deliverance.

The first stanza bids Israel look to the past. It recalls the miracle that God wrought at the very beginning of her history. When Abraham was but *one,* God called him and blessed him and made him *many.*

This passage takes on new meaning when we remember that Abraham and Sarah were living in Ur of the Chaldees when God first began to work his miracle in their lives. Although childless, they were to become the parents of an innumerable host (cf. Gen 15:1-6). Now to Abraham's descendants, who are in exile in the very land in which Abraham first received his call, there comes the command to look to Abraham and to Sarah and to have faith. Their future is not as hopeless as they imagine. God is about to work a miracle as he did in the long ago. Once again he will make a great nation out of only a few persons.

No matter how far we have come in our spiritual pilgrimage, it is always good for us to recall the beginning of our journey. Remembering our humble beginning ought to quench our pride and rekindle our faith in God. I know a professor in a theological seminary who keeps a pair of plow handles hanging in his office. This is a constant reminder to him of where his pilgrimage with God had its beginnings.

The appeal to the past (vv. 1-2) is followed by a promise for the future (v. 3). The Lord will comfort Zion and transform her devastated lands into a "garden of Eden." Joy and gladness will be found in her. These two words often appear together in the Old Testament (cf. Isa 35:10; 51:3, 11; Jer 33:11; Zech 8:19; Ps 51:8). This note of joy continues in the New Testament, which begins with joy over the birth of Jesus (Luke 2:13-14) and closes with the "hallelujah chorus" (Rev 19:6).

Israel was comforted in the midst of her servitude in Babylon. Likewise, Christian joy often arises out of persecution and tribulation. Christians know how to rejoice in persecution (Acts 5:41), in trials (1 Pet 4:12-13), in the loss of possessions (Heb 10:34), in poverty (2 Cor 8:2), in sorrow (2 Cor 6:10), and in all circumstances of life (Phil 4:4). Such joy is always the fruit of the Holy Spirit (Gal 5:22).

In the second and third stanzas the prophet deals with the transitoriness of the world as over against the permanence of God's salvation. Compare the command in verse 6 with that found in 40:26. In spite of all its majesty and apparent permanence, the universe in which we live is destined to vanish like smoke. Not only is nature transitory but so also are the nations of the earth that arise to oppress God's people (vv. 7-8). In such a world of change and decay only God remains constant. Therefore, his deliverance will be forever and his salvation to all generations (vv. 6, 8). The changelessness of God alone gives meaning to the changing human scene.

Israel's Prayer and God's Response (51:9–52:12)

One of the stylistic characteristics of this section is the repetition of words at the beginning of the different stanzas: "awake, awake" (51:9; 52:1); "I, I" (51:12); "rouse yourself, rouse yourself" (51:17); "depart, depart" (52:11).

The first "awake, awake" (51:9) is captive Israel's prayer to God. It is her response to the prophet's exhortation to look to the past (51:1-2). She is calling upon God to repeat the mighty acts of salvation that he performed when Israel came out of Egypt. She desperately longs for God to show himself as active in the present as he was in the long ago. Then her condition will be transformed to one of pure joy (v. 11).

There is an unusual tenderness in God's response to Israel's prayer (vv. 12-16). The repetition of "I, I" (v. 12) is a call for Israel to take her eyes off her difficulties and focus them upon her Lord and Maker. Why should she fear her oppressors? After all, they are mere human beings, made like grass and destined to die (v. 12). Furthermore, fearing other human beings causes one to forget God (v. 13). Those who are bowed down under the oppressor will soon be set free (v. 14). This promise is made on the authority of the Lord of hosts, the Creator of the universe, the covenant-God of Israel (vv. 15-16).

The repeated command in verse 17 is addressed to Jerusalem. The following verses describe the sad state of affairs within the city. Jerusalem is pictured as a woman staggering about in a drunken stupor. She holds a cup in her hand. It is called both the cup of wrath of the Lord and the bowl of staggering. She has drained this cup to the dregs (cf. 40:2). As she staggers about, none of her sons takes her by the hand to steady her or to guide her. The reason is that they, too, are drunk with the wrath of the Lord. They have passed out and lie in the streets like antelopes caught in a net.

To these who are drunk, though not with wine, God makes a promise. A new day is about to dawn for the disconsolate city. God is going to take the cup of staggering and the bowl of his wrath (note the reversal of the terms) from her hand and put them into the hand of her tormentors (vv. 21-23). These have long abused her and treated her with contempt, but the situation is going to be reversed and the tormentors will have to drink the cup of the Lord's wrath.

This promise is followed by a summons to Jerusalem to awaken and to put on her beautiful garments (52:1). The garments are a symbol of strength and of holiness. One can imagine the electrifying effect that the prophet's words must have had when he announced that the captive daughter of Zion was about to be set free (v. 2). Zion's glad morning was dawning in all of its glory.

Zion is going to be redeemed without money (vv. 3-6). This may mean either that God is going to pay her captors nothing for her release or that her redemption will cost her nothing.

Verses 7-12 provide an exhilarating climax to this section. It is no accident that the words of these verses have so often been set to music. They constitute a grand finale that calls for full orchestration. Surely they were meant to be sung!

In his imagination the prophet sees a runner speeding across the hills toward Jerusalem, loudly proclaiming the good news of peace and salvation (v. 7). As the runner approaches Jerusalem, he cries out, "Your God reigns!" The watchmen stationed on the walls catch the sound of his words and they raise their voices and sing together for joy. Before their very eyes they see the Lord returning to Zion, his ancient dwelling place.

No sooner had the watchmen begun to sing that the prophet bade the waste places of Jerusalem join in their song (v.9). At long last the Lord had comforted his people and had redeemed Jerusalem. Her salvation, furthermore, was but the prelude to an even greater act of redemption. The Lord was going to uncover his saving arm before the eyes of all the nations, and all the ends of the earth would see his salvation (v. 10). How beautiful upon the mountains are the feet of him who brings good tidings such as these!

The remarkable thing about this song's celebrating the victorious reign of God is that there was so much in the contemporary situation that seemed to contradict it. How could one believe that God reigned when Jerusalem still lay under the oppressor's heel? People of every generation face this same problem. How can one believe that God is king when evil seems to be enthroned on every hand? "Your God reigns!" was the message the waiting community of Israel needed to hear. The prophet believed that God was firmly in control of history, regardless of how much the circumstances at any given moment seemed to contradict this. His song was a song of praise to the Lord of history, a song sung in anticipation of the glorious reality we know as the kingdom of God.

It is generally accepted that verses 11-12 are a summons for the captive Jews to depart from Babylon (cf. 48:20-23; 55:12-13). A special command is given to those "who hear the vessels of the Lord" (v.

11). They are to remain ritually clean by purifying themselves and not touching any unclean thing.

It is taken for granted by most interpreters that this refers to the priests who bore the temple vessels that survived the destruction of Jerusalem. In other Old Testament passages where this expression is used, however, it is translated as "armor-bearers" (cf. Judg 9:54; 1 Sam 14:1, 6, 7, 12-14, 17; 16:21; 31:4-6; 2 Sam 18:15; 23:37). This could well be the meaning intended by the prophet in this passage as well. Those who marched in the army of the Lord and served as his armor-bearers must be free from all defilement.

This interpretation would relate this passage to the holy war passages found elsewhere in the Old Testament, especially in the accounts of the exodus out of Egypt (cf. 15:1-18). Once again God was going to deliver his people out of bondage. This deliverance would be like the exodus out of Egypt except in one important respect. This time Israel would not go out in haste, for God would go before her and behind her to guide her and to protect her (v. 12). God was her refuge and strength. Of whom should she be afraid?

Chapter Nine

ON THE EVE OF THE RETURN

52:13–55:13

The Travail and Triumph of the Servant (52:13–53:12)

This section opens with the fourth arid final Servant Song (52:13–53:12), by far the most significant of all the songs celebrating his mission and ministry. Here the servant is definitely treated as an individual, and a sharp contrast is drawn between his behavior and that of the Israelite nation as a whole. Cyrus had provided political redemption for Israel; the servant through his vicarious suffering and death would provide spiritual redemption.

Jesus deliberately modeled his ministry after the pattern laid down in the Servant Songs, especially this one. He saw himself as one who was sent to minister to others and to lay down his life for others. He refused to become a political Messiah like Cyrus (see 45:1), but chose instead to become a suffering Messiah, after the pattern of the servant. This conscious decision influenced not only his death and resurrection but also his entire ministry.

The disciples of Jesus and other early Christians had difficulty at first in comprehending this. If they had not had the Servant Songs to instruct them, they might never have understood why the one who was the object of their messianic hopes had to be crucified. Proof that they depended so heavily upon the fourth Servant Song to explain Jesus' suffering and death is found in the fact that portions of this song are quoted in all four gospels, as well as in Acts, Romans, Philippians, Hebrews, and 1 Peter. If for some reason the entire song were to be lost from the Old Testament, it could be almost completely reconstructed from the New Testament quotations. Nowhere in the Old Testament do we come so near the Cross of Jesus as here.

The song is composed of five stanzas, each of which is three verses in length. The following outline is suggested.

1. From humiliation to exaltation, 52:13-15.
2. The servant's unlikely beginning, 53:1-3.
3. The servant's vicarious suffering, 53:4-6.
4. The servant's sacrificial death, 53:7-9.
5. The servant's ultimate triumph, 53:10-12.

From humiliation to exaltation. In 52:13-15 we find a summary statement of the servant's rise from humiliation to exaltation. The speaker here is the Lord himself. He tells how the servant rises to heights of glory (52:13). His rise from humiliation to exaltation will be so unexpected that he will startle the nations (a better rendering than "sprinkle"), and kings will shut their mouths because of what they see (v. 15).

The servant's unlikely beginning. The opening question "Who has believed what we have heard?" is worded so as to receive a negative response (53:1). It was asked either by the Gentile kings referred to in 52:15, or by the Jews themselves, who express astonishment that such an unlikely person should have had such an unusual career.

God's ways are not our ways, and this is never more apparent than in the choice of those who will be his ministers and proclaim his word. He chose the Israelites when they were just a motley crew of slaves building the storehouses of the pharaoh of Egypt. He chose Moses and Jeremiah over their protests of unworthiness. He took two lowly shepherds, David and Amos, and made one a king and the other a prophet. Jesus chose his disciples from among tax collectors and fishermen. Paul wrote that God deliberately chooses the weak and the despised as his ministers, in order that no human being might boast in his presence (see 1 Cor 3:26-29).

Almost all possible misfortunes are attributed to the servant in 53:2-3. He is described as a stunted plant, struggling to survive in dry ground. His physical appearance is so grotesque that others turn away to avoid looking at him. Verse 3 has often been interpreted to mean that he was afflicted with the loathsome disease of leprosy, a disease that caused others to hide their faces in fear and revulsion. It is understandable, therefore, that he should be spoken of as "despised and rejected of men; a man of sorrows, and acquainted with grief" (53:3).

The servant's vicarious suffering. It has been said that the Old Testament reflects three levels of understanding regarding the meaning of suffering. At the first level, all sufferers are regarded as being sinners. This is the level of understanding reflected, for example, in the speeches of Job's friends. At the second level, some sufferers, such as, for example, Job and Jeremiah, are acknowledged to be saints. Their suffering remains an enigma both to themselves and to others. At the third level, some sufferers are regarded as saviors, because they willingly undertake to suffer for the sake of others. Their suffering has redemptive value because of its vicarious nature.

The servant's suffering fits this third category. The speakers can only say in amazement, "he has borne our griefs and carried out sorrows" (53:4). "He was wounded for our transgressions, he was bruised for our iniquities; upon him was the chastisement that made us whole, and with his stripes we are healed" (53:5). This all comes to a climax in 53:6 when the speakers freely confess that they had all gone astray like sheep, each turning to his own way, but that the Lord had laid upon his servant the blame that should have been theirs.

The servant's sacrificial death. The death of the servant is presented as the sacrifice of the innocent for the guilty (53:7-9). And yet it is a sacrifice that occurs outside the temple and its sacrificial system. The victim is an innocent person, and his sacrifice makes all other sacrifices unnecessary.

This must not be interpreted to mean that his sacrifice works automatically to remove sin. It is effective only for those who make it the means of their approach to God. It is effective only for those who confess, "He was wounded for our transgressions, and bruised for our iniquities." Such a confession is impossible apart from repentance. But when such a confession is made from the heart, it always leads to forgiveness.

A deliberative contrast is drawn in 53:6-7 between the crowd of sinners and the lone servant. The crowd confesses, "all we *like sheep* have gone astray" (53:6), but he, *like a sheep*, "is led to the slaughter" (53:7). But he still did not open his mouth, either to complain or to condemn. In the words of the spiritual, "He never said a mumblin' word." Other Old Testament sufferers either confessed their guilt and asked for forgiveness (see Pss 32:3-5; 38:3-4, 17-18; Isa 6:5), or else protested their innocence (see Job 34:6; Ps 44:17-18; Jer 15:18). In the servant we have a unique example of the innocent suffering in silence.

The servant's ultimate triumph. The most surprising thing about the story of the servant is that it does not end with his death. We learn first of all that his suffering and death were within the will and purpose of the Lord (53:10a). The Lord willed that his servant should be put to death, not because of any anger toward the servant but because of his love for sinners. The servant's death, therefore, was not the hopeless end of a tragic life, but rather the crowning event of that life, at least from God's standpoint. Death was the servant's greatest achievement, the achievement by which sinners could be restored to favor with God. The servant thus fulfilled his mission through his sacrificial death, but the results extended far beyond his death.

This song may have referred originally to some unnamed Israelite who would suffer and die on behalf of his contemporaries. If so, it is impossible to find anyone in the Old Testament times who even comes close to fulfilling this prophecy. When Christ came, however, this promise was transposed to a higher key and found its perfect fulfillment in him. He was the Suffering Servant of the Lord in a way no other person has ever been.

The Ecstasy of Freedom (54:1-17)

The day has drawn near for the exiles to depart for Jerusalem. The only word that could describe their sense of anticipation was the word ecstasy.

A population explosion. The first sign of God's favor upon restored Jerusalem would be an unexpected increase in its population (54:1-3).

It was unexpected because the city's present condition could be compared to that of a barren woman (v. 1), the same term as that used in Genesis 11:30 to describe Sarah, the barren wife of Abraham. Jerusalem is also described as "desolate" (v. ib), perhaps meaning that she felt that she had been forsaken by the Lord (see 50:1).

Suddenly the barren and desolate woman would find that her children were more in number than the children of a married woman (see 49:19-21). Like a desert nomad, she would need to enlarge her tent, by lengthening her cords and strengthening her stakes, in order to make room for all her family (54:2). Her children would spread out to the right and to the left, taking control of the Gentile nations, and settling the desolate cities of Judah (54:3). These verses are a useful commentary on the earlier statement in Isaiah 45:18 that the Lord created the heavens and the earth not to become a chaos but to be inhabited. He is always the God of order, and not of disorder. It is we who create disorder and barrenness.

On 31 May 1792, William Carey, a British Baptist minister who supplemented his meager income by cobbling shoes, preached an epoch-making sermon before a gathering of his fellow ministers at Kettering, England. He took as his text the words of Isaiah 54:2: "Enlarge the place of your tent, and let the of your habitation be stretched out; hold not back, lengthen your cords and strengthen your stakes." Carey's sermon was organized around two main points: (1) we should expect great things from God; and (2) we should attempt great things for God. In his sermon he made a passionate appeal for his listeners to accept responsibility for the worldwide mission of the church. Under the inspiration of his sermon, the Baptist Missionary Society was formed on 2 October 1792, an event that many regard as the initial step in the launching of the modern missionary movement. A year later, Carey himself was appointed by the newly formed missionary society to begin what proved to be a long and distinguished career as a missionary to Serampore, India. A biblical text written many centuries ago is still helping to shape modern church history.

An appropriate title for verses 4-8 would be "The Return of the Prodigal Wife." In language reminiscent of Hosea, the prophet describes Israel as the estranged wife of the Lord. She will soon forget the shame of her youth, that is, the time of her rebellion preceding the exile (v. 4). The period of the exile is described as a time when Israel was like a widow (v. 4) or a forsaken wife (v. 6). This time of reproach will also be forgotten and Israel will soon be restored to her Husband and Redeemer, who is none other than her Maker, the Lord of Hosts, the Holy One of Israel, the God of the whole earth (v. 5).

God's momentary wrath is contrasted to his great compassion and his everlasting love (vv. 7-8). The words translated "compassion" and "everlasting love" are among the most significant words in the Old Testament. The first of these describes God's pity for people in their frailty, misery, and helplessness. It is thus related more to human creatureliness than to sinfulness (cf. Ps 103:13-14).

The second word, *chesed*, is almost untranslatable. Miles Coverdale invented the word "lovingkindness" in an effort to translate it. The basic meaning is steadfastness or reliability. It describes the proper attitude that each party to a covenant should maintain toward the other. This is why the Revised Standard Version almost always renders it "steadfast love." In the majority of cases the King James Version reads "mercy." In 135 cases the Septuagint translates it by the Greek *eleos*, "mercy." The nature of *chesed* as mercy can be illustrated by the story of the Good Samaritan who "showed mercy" on the man who fell among thieves. It is the practical expression of helpfulness toward those whose only claim on our assistance is their misfortune.

The contrast between the momentary wrath of God and his everlasting love reminds one of similar words from the apostle Paul: "For this slight momentary affliction is preparing for us an eternal weight of glory beyond all comparison" (2 Cor. 4:17). And again in Romans 8:18: "I consider that the sufferings of this present time are not worth comparing with the glory that is to be revealed to us." Even though they may have to endure times of affliction, Christians, too, have a glorious future awaiting them.

Verses 9-10 describe God's everlasting covenant with his restored people. The meaning of verse 9 is brought out clearly in C. R. North's translation: "This is to me like the days of Noah over again, when I declared on oath that the waters of the flood should never again sweep over the earth; so now I swear that never again will I be wroth with you or rebuke you." God's promise is more secure than even the mountains (v. 10). Those who trust in him will never be put to shame.

The last section in this chapter (vv. 11-17) describes Zion's heritage of peace and prosperity. It is noteworthy that in this description of the rebuilding of Jerusalem (vv. 11-14) there is no mention of the temple. Verses 11-12 describe the physical splendor of the new Jerusalem, while verses 13-14 refer to her inward glory. In the time of her restoration she will have no cause for fear, for no weapon that is fashioned against her shall prosper (vv. 15-17). She will be secure from all of her enemies. "This is the heritage of the servants of the Lord and their vindication from me, says the Lord" (v. 17).

The Great Invitation (55:1-13)

The divisions of this chapter are

1. God's generosity, vv. 1-5.
2. A call to repentance, vv. 6-9.
3. God's unfailing word, vv. 10-11.
4. Homeward bound, vv. 12-13.

This chapter contains God's gracious invitation to a people bowed down under the bondage of Babylon. They were offered a great redemption that included spiritual sustenance (vv. 1-2), a renewal of the covenant (vv. 3-5), mercy and pardon (vv. 6-7), and a joyful return to the Land of Promise (vv. 12-13).

One of the marked features of this chapter is its frequent use of the imperative form of the verb. God commands his people to "come, buy, eat" (v. 1); "hearken, eat, delight yourselves" (v. 2); "incline your ear, come, hear" (v. 3); "seek, call" (v. 6); "forsake, return" (v. 7). While God's gifts can never be purchased or earned, this must not be interpreted to mean that they are dispensed automatically. In giving them, God gives nothing less than himself; in receiving them, man receives nothing less than God himself. God becomes the new center of his existence, and this is never an accidental occurrence. These imperatives prove that God's free redemption is not a divine act independent of human response.

God's invitation is given with a note of urgency. This sense of urgency is based on four vital truths.

God alone can satisfy the deep, inner needs of the human spirit (vv. 1-2). Water, wine, milk, and bread are but symbols of God himself. It is for God that the human spirit both hungers and thirsts, for man was created for fellowship with him. All who do not seek him are spending their substance for that which is not bread and wasting their energy on that which does not satisfy.

Israel's true destiny was to be a witness to the peoples and to call nations to acknowledge the sovereignty of her God (vv. 3-5). How could she be an effective witness unless she herself had responded to God's gracious invitation?

The opportunity for response had to be seized at once or it might be lost forever (vv. 6-9). "Seek the Lord while he may be found" (v. 6). In the hurried rush of life we are compelled to select only a very few of the things we might do or be. Both the responsibility and the consequences of choice belong to us.

God is faithful, and his promise never fails (vv. 10-11). This truth is expressed in language reminiscent of Isaiah 40:8: "The grass withers, the flower fades; but the word of our God will stand for ever."

> For as the rain and the snow come down from heaven,
>   and return not thither but water the earth,
> making it bring forth and sprout,
>   giving seed to the sower and bread to the eater,
> so shall my word be that goes forth from my mouth;
>   it shall not return to me empty,
> but it shall accomplish that which I purpose,
>   and prosper in the thing for which I sent it.   —vv. 10-11

The closing part of this chapter (vv. 12-13) should be compared with 48:20-21. Both are clarion calls for captive Israel to depart from Babylon. Why should she hesitate to follow her Lord? She had nothing to lose but her bondage.

You shall go out in joy,
    and be led forth in peace;
the mountains and the hills before you
    shall break forth into singing,
    and all the trees of the field shall clap their hands.
Instead of the thorn shall come up the cypress;
    instead of the brier shall come up the myrtle;
and it shall be to the Lord for a memorial,
    for an everlasting sign which shall not be cut off.

FOR FURTHER STUDY

Commentaries

Clements, R. E. *Isaiah 1–39*. The New Century Bible Commentary. Grand Rapids: Eerdmans Publishing, 1980.

Kaiser, Otto. *Isaiah 1–12*. Translated by R. A. Wilson. Old Testament Library. Philadelphia: Westminster Press, 1972.

_____. *Isaiah 13–39*. Translated by R. A. Wilson. Old Testament Library. Philadelphia: Westminster Press, 1974.

Kelley, Page H. "Isaiah," in *The Broadman Bible Commentary*, vol. 5. Nashville: Broadman Press, 1971.

Muilenburg, James. "The Book of Isaiah, Chapters 40–66," in *The Interpreter's Bible*, vol. 5. Nashville: Abingdon Press, 1956.

Scott, R. B. Y. "The Book of Isaiah, Chapters 1–39," in *The Interpreter's Bible*, vol. 5. Nashville, Abingdon Press, 1956.

Watts, John D. W. *Isaiah 1–33* and *Isaiah 34–66*. Word Biblical Commentary 24 and 25. Waco TX: Word Books, Publisher, 1985 and 1987.

Westermann, Claus. *Isaiah 40–66*. Translated by D. M. G. Stalker. Old Testament Library. Philadelphia: Westminster Press, 1969.

Other Studies

Achtemeier, Elizabeth. *Preaching from the Old Testament*. Louisville: Westminster/John Knox Press, 1989.

Blenkinsopp, Joseph. *A History of Prophecy in Israel*. Philadelphia: Westminster Press, 1983.

Brueggemann, Walter. *Hopeful Imagination: Prophetic Voices in Exile.* Philadelphia: Fortress Press, 1986.

Hayes, John H., and Stuart A. Irvine. *Isaiah the Eighth-Century Prophet: His Life and His Times.* Nashville: Abingdon, 1987.

Heschel, Abraham J. *The Prophets.* New York: Harper & Row Publishers, 1962.

Newsome, James D., Jr. *The Hebrew Prophets.* Atlanta: John Knox Press, 1984.

Von Rad, Gerhard. *The Message of the Prophets.* Translated by D. M. C. Stalker. New York: Harper & Row Publishers, 1967.

Seitz, Christopher R., editor. *Reading and Preaching the Book of Isaiah.* Philadelphia: Fortress Press, 1988.

Staton, Cecil P., Jr., editor. *Interpreting Isaiah for Preaching and Teaching.* Greenville SC: Smyth & Helwys Publishing, Inc., 1991.

Wilson, Robert R. *Prophecy and Society in Ancient Israel.* Philadelphia: Fortress Press, 1980.

LaVergne, TN USA
01 September 2009
156661LV00003B/164/P